5 MINUTES
MORE

THE MEMOIR OF A WORLD-CLASS MEDIUM

VAL HOOD

ISBN: 978-0-6456902-2-4 (EBOOK)
ISBN: 978-0-6456902-1-7 (PRINT)

Cover design by Sara Oliver

Book Design by HMDpublishing

Photography by Kieara Skie Photography

Important Note

This is my story as I remember it. I have not revealed details of names and locations. Nothing herein identifies any person unless permission has been acquired.

If you think you recognise yourself, know that this is not necessarily you. Over the 30 years of doing this work, I have had so many similar stories.

I have related these stories as they happened, including the key relationships I had with those individuals mentioned, and how they impacted me throughout the years.

Others who were present may remember things differently than me, and I honour that, too.

FOREWORD

There are many people, seen and unseen, who have helped to contribute to this book. They also continue to help me daily, and for that I am truly grateful.

I have been privileged to have had wonderful teachers guiding me, as well as students who have taught me so much. Thank you all.

I have listened to Spirit, who knew what was ahead for me, and as scary as that was a lot of the time, I trusted them – and here I am.

With love

from

Jac X

CONTENTS

CHAPTER I

Spirit and Me

How This All Started

I was 7 years old. A very quiet, shy, little blonde girl. And I saw dead people. I knew that I was different, but I couldn't quite put my finger on how. This made it hard to communicate with others outside of my family.

No one else, not even my family, had up to this point in my life talked to me about seeing or talking to these dead people, or talking to a real person who was not visible to others. I mean, how does one do that?

In school, I found myself standing at the fence that surrounded our playground at break time. The kids wouldn't talk to me, and I didn't know what to say to them. It was a lonely time for me, but as the eldest of four children at the time, when I got home I didn't need playmates and friends outside the family; we all lived under the same roof.

I didn't mention my visions either at home or school or who I was chatting to in the unseen world. I didn't want to look silly, crazy, or just plain mad.

We had moved into my grandparents' home after the death of my Nana. It was all very exciting, as we were moving, lock, stock, and barrel, from a small, two-bedroom flat to what seemed, to me at this tender age, to be a mansion.

Our flat had been tiny, with no garden, surrounded by concrete, and very cramped with six of us living in it.

Our new home had a huge garden at the back. It was like having our very own park, including beautiful trees that we happily spent time climbing in. There was also a secret garden, all the way at the very back, totally hidden from view, and accessed by a large private archway that had been built by my Grandad many years previously. From the time we moved in, this space provided all of us children with a safe place to hide, a place to hold clubs with friends and while away the summer hours. It was also far enough away from the house that if Mum was calling us, we could not hear her (or was it we just didn't want to hear her? After all, it would intrude on our magical space, where we loved to get lost in worlds of our own).

The garden at the front was awash with colour, and the heavy scent of the honeysuckle was intoxicating. I was fascinated by all of this, including the sounds of the swarms of bees, singing amongst the pretty plants.

This was a far cry from the tiny surrounds I had been used to, and from which I tried on several occasions to escape out of the windows. (I always got caught.) Dad always knew what I was up to. I wanted to explore the outside world, but that world was forbidden to me because the neighbourhood was very rough and not safe for kids. But here, in this safe space, I had a new playground to explore.

The garden was huge and seemingly went on forever. We had a side gate and no back access, which meant we could play all day and not get into any trouble or be bothered by anyone except our family. On the odd occasion, our neighbours on either side would pop their heads over the fence to say hello or ask us what we were up to or offer us a plate of cakes. Mum always knew where we were and we could not get into any major trouble.

Life was pretty normal to start with; our new school was only three doors away, and it seemed enormous compared to where we had come from. We all made new friends and life settled down to normality.

Initially my brother had a room of his own, which I was always very jealous of, and we three girls shared a room.

Grandad, whose bedroom was initially upstairs, was to now occupy one of the downstairs rooms. It was at the rear of the house, overlooking his beautiful garden. It had a bed, a sideboard with all his possessions. A very strange clock that he would wind daily – it made such a noise but was his pride and joy – as well as the biggest Bible I had ever seen. It was beautiful, very ornate, and had a brass hinge and clasp. He would let us look at it from time to time; dotted in amongst the pages were cards that my Nana had collected from our local church, marking her favourite passages and psalms. The family names had been written in with my Grandad's most ornate handwriting.

One of the drawers housed a Union Jack flag, carefully folded, which Grandad would get out from time to time to show us. There were also his medals and many spoons he had collected.

Sadly, Grandad had dementia and was lost in his own world most of the time. He had been a military band sergeant major, playing both clarinet and violin. Many times, he shared with us stories of those days. On other days, he would disappear into his own world of music in his head, conducting the band or playing his instruments, imaginary music playing loudly in his ears. He would 'whistle' and 'pom pom pom' all the time.

I knew my Nana, but as I was quite young and we lived a fair distance from her when she was alive; we didn't get to visit her that often. When we did go to see her, she would open her front door and the smells of beautiful cooking wafted out to hit us. Her kitchen was laden with all sorts of goodies she had baked – pies, cakes, scones, and biscuits, especially for us, piled high on plates in the kitchen.

She was always exuberant and animated in manner, with her arms going all over the place as she talked to us. "Oh, look at you all, how you've grown!" she would squeal with joy, greeting us all individually, her arms wrapping around us in giant, love-filled hugs. Each one of us getting special loving treatment. As she hugged me, I instantly got that warm, soft, familiar smell of her, like talcum powder. Even now, that memory fills me with warmth.

She was funny, loud, and always laughing. She had a funny accent that I didn't fully understand until many years later. She sang like a bird and smoked like a chimney, with a constant cigarette hanging from the corner of her mouth. I knew when I was with her that she loved us all dearly, and it showed in her excitement and constant chatter to us all. As she busied herself in her kitchen preparing the goodies for us, she never stopped talking.

Nana had held various jobs in her lifetime; nursing was one of them, and my dad would share her stories of her time in the mental hospital she worked at for a long time. He also spoke of her being such a great, kind, and caring person generally. He loved her very much, and his face would light up as he spoke of her, his smile and laughter showing that love. She was also loved within the community, and people often called on her to help them for many reasons; she was only too happy to help whenever she could. That was just her.

Before my beautiful Nana died at the age of 64, she had been working in a pie factory near where she lived. Recently, when doing some research on the family, I heard from someone who remembered her baking pies at home.

"My mum would send me to her house," the woman told me, "where I would knock on her door to buy a pie or two. They always smelled divine and were wrapped in a brown paper bag."

This was a side of Nana that I didn't know.

One day while working at the pie factory, she pulled a tray out from the oven, and it hit her in her breast. This sadly developed into breast cancer, which spread and ultimately caused her death.

On her deathbed, she asked my mum a question that must have been very difficult for Nana. "Would you take care of Grandad for me?" At the time, he was around 76, and because of his dementia could not look after himself or be trusted in the house on his own.

"Of course," Mum promised. "I will take care of him."

Nana's passing was not long after this promise was made, and our new adventures were about to begin. Mine were a little more interesting than the others.

What do you do when you start 'seeing' a dead person?

There were six of us children now, Mum having had two more girls. My brother was still in his own room, but our room now consisted of two sets of bunk beds and a single bed.

One particular night, we had all gone to bed at around seven, which was normal for us. It was bedlam in our household most of the time with so many of us. Bedtime was pretty full on, and it took forever for us all to settle.

We did eventually fall off to sleep but sometime later I suddenly found myself awake. I knew I'd been asleep for awhile as it was dark outside, and the house was very quiet.

What had woken me in the middle of the night?

I gathered my thoughts, rubbed my eyes, and adjusted to the darkness in the room. As I began to focus and search around the room, I saw her. My Nana. She was standing next to my sister's bed, but looking at me and smiling. My sister had been quite ill for a few days, and since my bed backed onto hers, I could see clearly what was happening. Still smiling, Nana turned to look at my sister, leaning over her to tuck her up in her bed in her usual gentle, caring way.

I didn't make a sound, but I felt fear constrict my throat. Nana looked very real to me, just like she had when she was alive – but she was dead. *How is this possible?*

It was strange – I was scared, but I sort of knew it was okay. I was safe, but the overwhelming fear still got to me. My emotions were all over the place. I pulled the covers up around my body to protect myself and just watched.

Everything seemed to be running in slow motion. No words were spoken, but we both understood the situation.

When she finished tending to my sister, Nana once again turned to me, smiled in her beautiful, warm way, then just faded away. She was gone!

I lay there for some time, terrified of what had just happened. Trying to make sense of it all. The experience had really spooked me. How did a 7-year-old cope with seeing her Nana, when her Nana was DEAD?

On top of this, everyone else was still asleep. No one had stirred. *Why is it just me?*

I eventually drifted back to sleep, but the haunting apparition stayed with me for quite some time. I still felt I could not share this with anyone – what would they think of me?

How was this possible? What was happening to me? Was it my imagination, or was I dreaming? Why was she there? What was going on? Why was I seeing these things? Was I crazy? What did all this mean?

I might have only been a child, but I wasn't stupid. I knew this was very real, but I couldn't answer the questions running through my brain.

Despite my terror, I kept Nana's appearance to myself. How could I explain what had happened? How could I put it into words?

The following day, my sister was so much better. Her fever had gone, and she was running around as if nothing had been wrong with her. *Did Nana have something to do with that?* I would like to think she did.

It was hard coming to terms with something I didn't fully understand and couldn't share. My fear was very real. I truly didn't know what to do. I had to think. I had to come up with a plan to protect myself somehow. At the time, I thought the plan I came up with was ingenious.

I organised a nightly ritual to help protect me. *Do I need protecting?* I was still frightened. Yes, I know this was my Nana, but I couldn't explain why I was seeing her after she had died.

This was the plan I hatched: I would close the bedroom curtains, lifting the bottoms of the curtains up onto the window ledge. Then I sat my dolls up on top of the curtain on the ledge.

My thinking was that if someone came in through the window, all the dolls would fall off and wake not just me but also all my sisters.

I tried to be thorough. *What else can I do?*

The wardrobe: I would open the door, check inside, make sure there was nothing lurking in that internal darkness, and then shut and lock the door.

The only other thing I could think of was under the beds. Before I got into my own bed, I would check underneath all the beds in our room just to make sure there was nothing hiding there that could jump out in the darkness of the night.

Once I had completed all my little checks, I would jump into my bed, bury my whole body, including my head, under the covers, and stay there till morning. I was not coming out for anyone or anything.

The difficult thing with this part of the plan was that we only had one toilet, and that was downstairs at the furthest point from my room. The journey to the toilet would have been in pitch darkness. My fear of leaving my room in the dark was too big for me and I decided that I would not venture out. It was around the time of first seeing Nana that I started wetting the bed.

These visits from Nana continued throughout the next few years. She showed herself to me at different times. I would be standing in the garden, or playing in my bedroom, or even having dinner with the rest of the family and there she would be, this smiling, glowing lady, standing watching me. When I say glowing, I mean it – she literally glowed.

I watched my brothers and sisters to see if they, too, were seeing things. But no one said a thing. *Am I the only one?* I tried really hard to keep an eye on what they were all up to, but nothing caught my eye, and certainly no one else mentioned it happening to them. It appeared that I was the only one seeing her. No one else acknowledged her presence. There was never a glimmer to suggest that they had seen anything out of the ordinary.

Given this, I was terrified to mention Nana's appearances to my family, though whether this was due to my fear or my shyness, I wasn't sure. I decided to keep all of her 'visits' to myself, as I didn't want them to think I was mad or going crazy, which it felt like to me. It's strange to think back on how little 7-year-old me coped with all of this. I never knew when Nana was going to appear or where, meaning I was never prepared, and she always surprised me.

Some of my most memorable visions of Nana occurred between 12 and 16 years old.

One significant sighting of Nana was when I was a very hormonal 16-year-old. I had been arguing with my dad. We were always having run-ins and this day was no different. I don't remember what I had supposedly done but he was shouting at me. I needed to escape. I stormed up the stairs, hitting each stair like I was an elephant. I headed straight for the bathroom and locked myself in.

Once I had locked the door, I turned to look at my tear-stained face in the mirror. Imagine my utter surprise when in that mirror was both my face AND my Nana's face. *Oh, my goodness, what is this?* My breath caught in my throat, and I stopped dead in my tracks. The fear froze me for a moment in time.

Is this really happening? I turned to check there was nothing on the door that was creating Nana's image in the mirror. But no, the door was just as plain and white as ever.

Turning to look into the mirror, she was still there, smiling at me with that recognisable, beautifully glowing face.

I had reached my limit. I couldn't cope with her strange visitations anymore. I had had enough. I didn't understand them or why she was there. I needed to do something, to say something to her and to Spirit.

I found myself standing on the landing in the middle of our house. With hands raised to the heavens, I very ceremoniously had words with 'them' and 'her'.

I had not spoken to Spirit before in this way, and I don't know why it occurred to me to talk to them now, but I felt instinctively it was the right thing to do. My hands up in front of me as if in a sort of prayer, talking to the air, giving them a piece of my mind. Making them understand my fears.

I told them in no uncertain terms, "I know you are here, but I don't understand what's going on and I'm scared. Please, can you go away and leave me alone?"

I continued, "I promise you that when I understand what is happening to me, and have more knowledge and have lost my fear, I will let you back in." These words just flowed from my mouth as if it was the most normal thing in the world.

I instinctively knew that this was the right thing to do. I realised 'they' were there with me, and I was having a conversation with 'them'. I was telling them clearly that I was scared. I wanted them to listen and stop scaring me. I wanted to understand what was happening and why.

To my surprise, that is exactly what happened. I told them how I was feeling, and they respected my wishes. From that day forward, they appeared to have left me alone.

I have obviously learned much more over the years. I do believe when working with Spirit that there is a mutual respect.

It was incredible; I had no more sightings of Nana until was in my 30s. I just got on with my life, doing normal things like getting married, having children, travelling, working, and more.

From this young age, I had been using my mediumistic abilities and just hadn't realised it. It just came naturally to me; I instinctively knew how to help someone.

When I was 12, a boy that I really liked in my class was told that his dad had been killed. It was such a shock to us all in the class that day, but more so for me as he worked at the same company as my dad. They both drove trucks. Steve's dad had been killed in a truck accident.

He was not at school for a few weeks, and not only did I miss him, but I wanted to help him in some way. When he returned to school, I was able to do that.

You find that when someone close to you dies, people don't know how to talk to you about it. They change the subject or cross the road or stop calling you. I have spoken to many people who say that's the worst thing anyone can do.

Instinctively, I knew that it was right to ask Steve about his dad, what had happened, what sort of man and dad he was. He loved that I was interested. We would sit on the grass at the edge of the playground, away from the other kids, and spend as much time as we could chatting about his dad. He was happy in those moments, and we did it often. That feels like it was a special time to me. I was beginning to work with Spirit even though I didn't realise it at the time.

Nana's initial visit was about giving my sister healing because she was sick. Healing isn't limited to people who had medical training when they were here in the physical – anybody can do it. Most Spirit communication and visitations are about healing and helping. It's part of their role from the Spirit realms, to come back and help us all where they can. Whether they are family or not, the healing part of the communication has a very big part to play. I will talk about the healing aspects more in Chapter 14.

My Nana was there to help me! To show me that it was okay to see dead people. Spirit would not harm me, especially not my Nana; she loved me. I was slowly learning that this applied to all Spirit who came into my life; they loved me and cared for me. I was being prepared for something bigger.

Many years after I had started training to be a medium myself, I found out from family that my Nana was also a medium – in fact, she was a tea leaf reader, and a very good one at that. People would come from far and wide to visit her for her spiritual insights. I never understood why I had not been told; it would have made my life so much easier and much less scary. Perhaps there was, even in those days, fear or stigma attached to all things spooky or ghostly.

No wonder she wanted to be around me to help me. She knew I was to become a medium.

I was not scared now, I was made to feel the comfort of their presence, there was nothing to be frightened of. My Nana had loved me. Why should I be scared?

These things are always easy in hindsight, but at the time I hadn't a clue what was happening. I just knew I was scared – very scared.

Many times, after a demonstration of mediumship, people come up to me after watching me work say things like, "You have a lovely older lady by the side of you" and "I could see this smiling red-headed lady behind you." They have been able to describe her smooth skin, red hair with a silver streak through the front, glasses, and that incredible smile, and I know it's her; I know that Nana is working alongside me. That gives me incredible amounts of joy and comfort. I feel her love constantly around me.

I believe now that Nana was not trying to frighten me as a child. She knew I had the gift and was trying to help me. That's why it's so important to be able to talk about such things.

ALL of us are born with the ability to connect to Spirit. We are also given the healing gift; these are the most natural gifts to be given. It's sad, then, that the big, bad world takes over, usually around the age of 8, when for the majority of us that wonderful natural spiritual ability is taken away.

Parents of children who see Spirit may not be aware of Spirit themselves or understand what is happening. I have heard of many stories of parents who tell their children, "It's imaginary friends" or "You're making it up" or "Don't be stupid."

I find this disappointing. I would love to educate people to have more of an understanding of Spirit so that when their children are coming out with spooky things, they can either find someone who can help the child or just talk to their child themselves and ask questions like, "Who are they?" "What do they talk to you about?" or show them family pictures of people who have passed and ask, "Do you recognise them?"

Children are naturals as they have no pre-conceived ideas yet. They need to know that if there is someone there like 'a man in the cupboard' or 'the lady who sits on my bed at night' that it's okay; they're not going to hurt you. They want to play, comfort, help, tell you they saw you score a goal in soccer, just like a normal person would do.

Some people have Spirit come to them for the first time after a major trauma or tragedy like the death of a loved one and they suddenly start to see 'dead people'. This again is natural. Spirit are aware of your feelings and want to help.

These people are coming to tell you "I'm okay, I'm out of pain, I am still here with you, don't be sad, there was nothing more you could have done." This is all very normal.

When they were here on earth, our Spirit loved ones would have taken good care of us and loved us. Their energy, essence, soul, memories and love continue to stay around us. They watch over us and help us when and where they can.

The body is the physical vehicle we use in our earthly existence to carry us through this physical life. When we are done with our physical body, Spirit continues to exist in a different dimension, on a different vibration. The physical body is no longer needed. The body is what perishes, not the soul.

Our Spirit continues to live on after our physical death.

Spirit knows before we come into this world what our work and our life lessons are going to be; this is a contract that must be fulfilled to allow our spiritual progress. The details of that contract are forgotten by the conscious mind when we arrive here on earth.

It's not just a case of us being chosen by them; we were also part of that choice.

How did Spirit get me to the next stage of working with them?

I believe there were a lot of earthly experiences I was meant to have for me to work with Spirit. However, I was merrily going along on a different path before Spirit brought me back on track – but I now had what I needed to be able to do that work.

CHAPTER 2

My Family and Childhood

At this point, I feel that it's important to give a bit of my background, in order to show my commitment to all the experiences I have had in my past that paved the way for my future.

I thought I knew what I wanted, but Spirit knew what I needed.

I wanted to be the musician, but Spirit needed me to be the medium!

I was born in Billericay, Essex, in February 1955. Interestingly, I recently heard that most of the best mediums come from Essex. I moved to Wales when I was about 18 months old.

I was the eldest of six children, five girls and one boy. When I was 8, I was tiny and very shy – until I discovered I had this amazingly powerful voice. When I first started singing, I didn't understand where this voice came from.

At school we had to sing a lot. The teachers picked up on my strong voice straight away and I was chosen to sing solo parts for all sorts of events held throughout the year. When I joined groups like the Brownies, I got picked to sing for special occasions, such as Sunday Parade services.

Wales is a beautiful, very special country. The people here are passionate about many things – their heritage, culture, and their love of music. They hold Eisteddfods (competitions), which are held in all schools as well as for adults. This tiny country certainly loves its musical heritage.

Rugby is high on the list, too; they are a very competitive nation. Singing again shows up here with cheering on their teams.

Mining was at one point the mainstay of Welsh living, and when work finished, the men would head to the pubs, where again the singing took place. There are many choirs in Wales and male voice choirs are predominant.

The people here also have a profound sense of family and community. In the 1800s, the Welsh language was banned, and Welsh books were burned. This was at a time when the English bought up and took over the mines. Perhaps this fierce passion stems from these times.

In all the schools I was connected to, we were encouraged to sing and participate in music in some way or other. I feel very fortunate to have been surrounded with this amount of competitiveness and the passion for all things Welsh.

Little did I know at the time that I too had this internal need to perform.

My family was all very musical. My granddad on Dad's side was a violin and clarinet player in a military band and had attended military music schools in India. Grandad proudly showed off the photographs of himself in his uniform, in the orchestra and military band. He was a tall, thin, proud, and very handsome man. Later in life, after leaving the military, he played in orchestras in Cardiff, which was the town I grew up in.

Dad had a beautiful voice like Frank Sinatra. Very powerful and melodic. He always sang with such passion. At the age of 18 he was conscripted into the army. One of his postings was to Korea in the 1950s. On the ships going to and from there, he used to entertain the troops by singing. He had in fact been offered a professional career in music, which he turned down. I didn't know the reason behind this decision.

His brothers and sisters all sang or played musical instruments or both. Family gatherings, such as Christmas, were always so much fun. To hear everyone participating was great, but for me to watch my dad sing was mesmerising. He had the voice of an angel, and everyone sat rigid listening with such intent as he sang.

My mum's family came from the London area and were true 'Cockneys'. They too were musical, playing various instruments and singing. My nan loved to tell us tales of the family congregating around 'the old Joana' (Cockney rhyming slang for piano) and entertaining themselves with a 'good old knees up.' They were a large family, and Mum remembers from being a little girl how much fun these events were.

Dad told stories of my Nana and her singing. In fact, right up until she died, she would sit in her bed, really sick, cigarette in hand – yep, still smoking like a chimney – telling funny stories, laughing heartily, and singing at the top of her voice.

My voice emerged out of this background. When I was singing with others at school, I would out-sing them all. Even though I was incredibly shy, once I started singing, I would get lost in a different world. The world of music became a passion of mine. I was always nervous before I had to sing, but once I started, it wasn't me up there, it was my voice. I was almost hiding behind the voice.

Later, at the age of 10, my dad acquired a pianola. He used to run a milk round, and one day a customer told him she was getting rid of it and asked if he could find a use for it. He was a very practical man, could build up and knock down anything. He said yes and prepared to move it to our house. He loved the idea of anything for free – but a piano, that was quite special.

He took the whole thing apart there and then brought it home on his milk wagon. I remember the excitement when he got home that day. You could almost hear the poor milk wagon groaning under the weight of the instrument, resting dangerously low to the ground.

We all watched as he unloaded and re-assembled this monstrosity. It was rather large. We had no idea what it was initially but when it was finished, it was gorgeous, and we were all very excited to have a piano.

It, however, didn't look like the pianos I had seen at school. This one had a roll of paper in a little cupboard at the front. There were several of these rolls that came with the piano, and it turned out they were music scrolls of different songs.

It was great fun for all of us, as one would sit on the stool pretending to play and two of us would sit underneath on the floor pressing with all our might on the enormously heavy pedals. These pedals made the paper roll turn. The paper had little holes dotted all over it and this was how the tunes were made, like a musical box. We spent many happy hours doing this, pretending to be wonderful musicians. We did eventually all learn to play properly.

I was fascinated by the piano and would play ours at home all the time. Well, it wasn't playing as such, more like tinkering.

When I was 10 years old, our music teacher, Mr Jellings, would play a certain tune that I loved. It was a very haunting piece. I wanted to see if I could play the same tune by ear. I decided to sneak into the school hall and try to play it.

I was thrilled as I had done it, however, as I sat happily playing, the door of the hall opened and in walked Mr Jellings. I was terrified. I thought I was in the biggest amount of trouble I'd ever been in. I never got into trouble.

He just looked at me and said, "Follow me."

I got frog-marched back to his classroom. He did not say a word, and the walk seemed to take forever. We eventually arrived; he sat stern faced at his desk, took out a piece of paper, and scribbled something on it. Then, still without speaking, he stood up and went to his music cupboard at the back of the room. After rummaging through it, he pulled out a pile of books. He handed them all to me and sent me home with instructions to give the note to my mum.

I was almost in tears at this point, thinking I was going to get into big trouble when I got home.

I arrived back home and did as I was told. My mum took the note and read it in silence, then raised her eyes to look at me. I wanted the earth to swallow me up; it was unbearable. Mum just had to look at us in a certain way and we knew we were in trouble. This was the look I was getting now.

Finally she spoke, and I was relieved as she told me that Mr Jellings had heard the musical potential I had. In the note he had asked my mum if she could get me piano lessons. We were fairly poor at the time, and this would have stretched the budget beyond her planning, however, the books he had kindly given me were a start, each of them being of such value.

I was relieved that I was not in trouble that day, and yes, Mum arranged for me to have piano lessons.

This was the beginning of my musical performing. Although still shy, I was quite a strong character in lots of ways, and if I wanted to do something, I usually did and succeeded at it.

Dad encouraged us all to sing and would get my brother and sisters performing at Christmas family parties. Boxing Day was traditionally the day when all our families got together, and everyone had to get up and do their party piece. It was very exciting each year, with the oldies getting up and singing the same songs that us kids used to laugh at every year. There were the voices, the violin, piano – even the spoons would be played. It was very entertaining.

Dad trained us for weeks beforehand and, like the Von Trapp family from *The Sound of Music*, the six of us would get up to sing. As each person had their turn, I could feel the nerves building up in me. We didn't want to let Dad down. We sang songs like 'Moon River' and 'Climb Every Mountain'. When we had finished, we were happy when the family applauded us enthusiastically.

I began to sing publicly from the age of 8. I was in the school choir, church choir, Ely Girls' Choir, which was our local choir, and Brownies, where I sang at their monthly special services.

The Ely Girls' Choir consisted of approximately 30 girls and had a fabulous choir master, Ieuan Lewis. He was one of our schoolteachers and worked closely with Mr Jellings, who was also my form teacher. These two wonderful teachers put on many school productions together.

They had a fantastic reputation as teachers; they were both lovely, warm, caring men who wanted to share their love of music and generally their love of education in all forms.

Mr Lewis had great visions for his choir. His vision originally was for a boys' only choir similar to the Vienna Boys' Choir. Unfortunately, the boys at our school were not interested. However, there were numerous girls who WERE interested. Many girls were auditioned, and the Ely Girls' Choir was formed.

He was such a perfectionist, which made for a perfect choir. We travelled extensively throughout England and Wales. Those bus trips were special, with lots of fun and laughter and obviously lots of singing. We would hijack the microphone and take it in turns to do a part. This made the long journeys go much quicker and we all loved every minute of it.

He was very fair, too, and gave us all an opportunity to shine, taking turns to do a solo or duets to stand out in the front at concerts.

One young girl had sneaked through somehow who could NOT sing. Mr Lewis didn't have the heart to get rid of her, and she became the reader of exquisite poetry or segments from Shakespearean plays. He had created a very big part for her to play.

One year he entered us in the Llangollen International Eisteddfod, which is held annually in Wales. The year we entered, there were 36 choirs from around the world competing. We would walk around the grounds of the festival, watching some of these choirs practicing; they were brilliant. We were aged 10–17, and these other choirs were all adults.

We happened to be the youngest group entering that year. Our segment was to be in the main marquee, which was enormous, as was the stage, and there seemed to be hundreds of people inside. We sang our hearts out, and then came the announcements. "Ely Girls' Choir is placed 6th."

A great achievement, Mr Lewis told us. None of us could believe it. It was a great reflection on him as our musical director and on us as singers.

In Llangollen, we stayed in a run-down wooden school hall. We slept on camp beds that I think must have belonged to the war era. They were old and smelled funny. There was no hot water, and it was freezing.

At night the youngest of us had to go to bed when the older girls were allowed to stay up and go out.

The early-to-bed girls did not want to miss out on the fun, so we created our own entertainment. We decided on various ideas, such as a concert where each had to do their own party piece. We were all excited, deciding who was going to do what, and had so much fun and hilarity at putting this all together.

There we all were in our nighties with scripts, song sheets, and props in hand, and we put on our spectacular show. There were such a variety of performances.

I decided to impersonate Sir Harry Secombe, who was a rather large famous Welsh singer. In order for me to look the part, I stuffed a pillow up my nightie, stood on the camp bed that acted as my stage, and sang to my heart's content, 'If I ruled the world...' And then into the room came Mr Lewis, who had been alerted by all the noise and wanted to investigate.

As he walked through the door, we were all extremely shocked. For me the timing couldn't have been better, as my camp bed ripped, and with such panache, I went hurtling to the ground, feathers flying everywhere from the burst pillow still up my nightie. The girls all burst into raucous laughter while I spat feathers.

Thankfully Mr Lewis saw the funny side of this, too, and proceeded to ask us what we had all been doing. He was impressed with our impromptu concert.

Strange that coming forward more than 50 years, I found myself performing a mediumship demonstration at the theatre built in memory of Sir Harry Secombe, as he became known. It was the Secombe Centre in Surrey, where I later was to live.

I still find it hard to believe that this little girl, who was painfully shy, always wanted to be centre stage, singing, or playing an instrument. I certainly was not a precocious child.

~❖~

At the age of 9, and with only a year to go at junior school, I was especially excited to arrive at school to hear news that the school had been given funds by the local council to buy violins. To my dismay and total disappointment, I was told that only those children who had two full years plus left in the school would be allowed to have these lessons. I was heartbroken. I WANTED to learn. Why couldn't I?

I went home that day in tears. Mum was shocked to see me like this. "What on earth has happened?" she asked. I relayed the whole story to her through my sobs, runny nose, and tears.

She promised me that she would do her best to help, and the following day she came up to the school and pleaded with Mr Jellings to let me be part of the violin group.

It worked – Mum was a miracle worker. And hey presto, I was told that I would be allowed to join the new violin group.

I also made a point of telling Mr Jellings, "I promise to support the school and the new orchestra for as long as I can." I kept my promise to him and the school until I was 19, when I moved to Germany to live. It was such fun coming back regularly to play with all the little kids.

I went on to play the violin for the Cardiff Junior and Senior Orchestras, reaching first desk position, which was quite scary as you are right in the front line. First desk is where the leader of an orchestra sits. I was very proud of my achievements.

I learned to played various other instruments including guitar, piano, banjo (a little), recorder (all sizes), and glockenspiel, which is like a xylophone. I was convinced at this time that I would end up as a singer or performer of some description as music had become so important to me.

I feel lucky to have lived in Wales, the land of song, and to be a part of a school that was rich with music and two amazing teachers who had that zest for both the music and teaching.

Every opportunity I had to be up on that stage, in front of people, I took with gusto. I would sing, play, narrate Welsh poems, sing accompanied and unaccompanied. I remember all the excitement with the practice sessions that were held in different parts of the school.

Our schools also taught Welsh as a second language, and I was able to speak the language quite well. Once a week we would have a Welsh assembly, and I would always be picked to read the Bible in Welsh, which was quite an honour.

The orchestra was a big part of our school assemblies. I would hop between singing, playing various instruments, and reading. It's quite funny, thinking back on it now, but I just loved every minute of it.

I look back on this now, and I don't know how I got up in front of people and performed as I did. I was always full of nerves, but I did it. I feel as if I was hiding behind the voice, the violin, the orchestra, the piano. It was never Val the person.

My spiritual work is the same; I am extremely nervous before I perform, but once I get up there and start connecting to Spirit, Val gets pushed to one side. Then, as soon as I've, finished the nerves jump back in. Again, I just get totally lost in the performance. I am lost in the moment.

A friend of mine who came to a theatre performance recently said that he could not believe that although I was extremely nervous and insecure before and after a performance, the bit in the middle was carried out with such confidence. I said to him, "That's because it's not me doing it, it's them!" Again, being lost in the performance, totally submerged in what I was supposed to be doing. I love that other people can see this, too.

How does all the above fit in with my work now? I believe that all my stage training has helped me with my mediumship work on many levels, not least being able to stand confidently on stage and to project your voice for people to hear you. Many of the halls I have worked in over the years have had very poor acoustics.

The singing training has therefore been invaluable, as among other things it taught me to project my voice to the back of the room in order for everyone in that hall to be able to hear.

As I said at the beginning of this chapter, Spirit knew what I needed.

CHAPTER 3

How I Became a Medium

All of us are guided by Spirit; there is no doubt about that. Over hundreds of years there has been much study of Spirit. There is too much proven evidence to be found in the many books and studies undertaken in the days of our pioneers, mentioned later on in this chapter.

Our own minds create the blockages. This is due to the fear of the unknown, of not knowing what is happening. But this is the most normal ability. We should learn to trust it more and realise how much good it can do us and how helpful we could find it.

There are many grounded people who work with Spirit. These people don't just accept what is happening with Spirit; they question, search for answers, and seek out others in order to talk about or share their experiences.

Then there are those I have come across who work with Spirit who are really "airy fairy".

The dictionary meaning of this is 'impractical and foolishly idealistic'.

These types of people have their heads in the clouds and believe everything and anything without question. They are those people who say, for instance, "Spirit said...." or "Spirit told me to..." They use Spirit to make all their decisions for them rather than making their own personal choices.

I think it is important to be guided and directed by Spirit in a very grounded way. They are here to guide us and help us where they can, not to take over and do it all for us. That would defeat the object of being sent here to learn that next lesson. We need the experiences and Spirit will make sure that we are doing what we need.

We make the decisions, but Spirit is helping and guiding us. They can step in when they think our judgement is clouded and give us that extra nudge.

We must be proactive in our own lives. We make our own choices, but knowing that we are being guided is very reassuring.

I have had many pushes and shoves in directions I was not expecting, and these have turned out to be quite remarkable at times. I can certainly say that life working with Spirit can be very interesting and exciting indeed.

I know that they have helped, and often I have reacted with, "Well I didn't realise I could do it that way," or "Wow, I didn't see that one coming." I have experienced this with regard to my relationships, business, homes, and friendships.

Spirit do try very hard, and they must get a bit fed up with us sometimes when we just don't get it or see it. They must feel like they have to hit us over the head with a sledgehammer.

Spirit tried very hard to get me to the spiritualist church where they knew I would get the help I needed. It took a while for that to get through to me, but when I did, it was life changing.

Life was a very dark place for me at that time. I was in a very unhappy marriage, had three young children, and had recently moved from my hometown in Wales to the large metropolis of London. This was all totally different and so alien to me, a completely different way of life.

I came from a very small, sleepy, seaside village, where everyone knew everyone as well as all their business. Then, here I was, in a huge city that was fast, dirty and noisy, with buildings that almost engulfed you. Wherever you looked, tall buildings seemed to swallow you up. To add to this, I found the people here very unfriendly and uncommunicative.

No one spoke to you. This was very different from the Welsh village overlooking the sea, surrounded by green pastureland, rolling hills, grazing sheep, and the ocean, where we all spoke to one another.

I had also moved from a large house overlooking the beautiful Welsh coastline to a very small two-bedroom flat. London felt like a concrete jungle by comparison.

There was a total of 32 flats in our complex, and I was shocked to find that when you passed your neighbours on the front path or even when hanging out the washing, they would lower their heads to avoid acknowledging you. They just shut down. A wall was put up. How strange this was to me.

My whole life felt squashed up and controlled. In every way. It was horrible. I thought I had made the right decision in moving my family to London, but I had come away from everything familiar to live in a place where I knew nothing at all.

I had left all my friends and family behind to follow the man that I loved to London, but the city was big, cold, and unfriendly. Nothing made any sense. Making new friends for me was impossible because, in my unhappy marriage, I was not allowed to make friends.

Spirit was about to show me that the time was right for them to consciously come back into my life. Something was about to change, and it needed to.

It was mid-winter in the UK and pretty bleak, and my relationship was going from bad to worse. I was letting myself down and, more importantly, letting my children down. I was very sick; some days I just could not breathe.

I feel the breathing was a reflection of the life I now found myself in. I was stifled and had no voice of my own.

There I was, feeling unbelievably low and in a real state of despair. It was not a good feeling. *What can I do? Who can I turn to?* And then, as clear as a bell, I heard a voice in my head.

It was there, talking to me, telling me, "Go and find a spiritualist church."

There are many religions and types of churches, but the spiritualist church is different.

Spiritualist churches are places of worship for those who practice spiritualism. A spiritualist service is usually conducted by a medium. Generally, there is an opening prayer, an address, the singing of hymns, and finally a demonstration of mediumship. Healing circles may also be part of the formal proceedings.

A medium is a person who can communicate with Spirit and pass messages and information from them to us.

Prayers are said to Spirit. In spirituality we believe that God is not a man who sits on a chair in heaven looking down upon us, like a lot of us are taught when we are children, but is instead the life force within us all.

The sermon could be inspiration from your daily life or spiritual books you read or could be directly channelled from Spirit.

The most important difference is, halfway through a service the medium makes those connections to Spirit and brings through their messages of love. They bring information to the audience from their loved ones in Spirit. Evidence of who they are.

At first, I didn't act, but Spirit's message was still there. It got louder and clearer, persistently pushing me to "find a spiritualist church." Then, one day, I plucked up the courage and picked up the phone. I called the council and said, "I am looking for any spiritual churches in the area; can you help me?" I was so desperate; the council lady I spoke to must have been able to hear the desperation in my voice.

What have I got to lose? I thought. It was such an unknown for me.

Maybe this was the lifeline I was looking for at the time, something for me to hold on to. I desperately wanted to believe this was the case – I had nothing else.

This was the end of the line for me otherwise.

I got the numbers of three churches that were fairly local, but one of these happened to be in an area that I was familiar with, as my boys went to school nearby. I looked up the details of their services, and the next Sunday I went along to West Wickham Spiritualist Church. I was full of trepidation, scared, miserable, unhappy...and what a mess I looked.

My unhappiness showed very obviously in my physical appearance. I had always prided myself on the way I dressed, which was impeccable. I worked in offices and wore up-to-the-minute suits with beautiful, heeled shoes and the latest hairstyles.

It wasn't just the appearance of my clothes – it was my physical body, the way I carried myself. I looked as if I had the world upon my shoulders, weighing every part of me down, threatening to bring me to the ground. Most of the time it felt as though I was dragging myself along.

Sunday arrived, and I walked shyly into the church building. I had no confidence, my hair was greasy, I had on an old Barber (wax farmers) jacket, and leggings with holes in them. No make-up. My lungs were getting worse, and I was struggling to breath all the time. I looked a total wreck.

West Wickham was a purpose-built church. I walked in through large wooden doors and as I entered, I was overcome by this strange feeling. *What is that?*

I had learned to just exist, to put up with the pain in my body, the shortness of breath, and the total lack of energy. I didn't know what was happening to me.

I was sad from the inside out, and it showed in my whole demeanour. But I didn't care; I was surviving, and that was all I could do at the time.

There I was, a crumpled wreck, sitting very guardedly in the back row of the church, trying to be inconspicuous. I felt very alone, unsure, and unhappy.

The church filled up slowly, and then we were all called to order; the service was about to begin. There must have been roughly 70 people in the hall, all of them strangers to me, making me feel lonelier. Though a few people did come up and greet me with a cheery 'hello' when I first walked in, I didn't feel like responding.

The service started, and suddenly it felt like I was being given a giant hug. I had never experienced anything like this before. *What is happening?* It wasn't physical, but it was certainly there – I could feel it, I could sense it, I knew it. I felt loved, welcome, and warm.

The service consisted of prayers and songs, which happened to have the most meaningful words. Very meaningful to me, anyway.

There were two people on the stage at the front of the hall – the chairperson and the medium.

The medium gave a talk that stopped me in my tracks. It felt like he was speaking to me personally. Almost as though everyone else in the hall had disappeared, as though I was the only one sitting there and he was speaking all these beautiful meaningful, heartfelt words TO ME.

I had never experienced anything like this ever before. It felt magical and so wonderful. I had an incredibly strange feeling of suddenly belonging. A feeling that I was in the right place. I was safe; I was meant to be sitting there. I knew that, but how did I know?

Then the next part of the service started, and the medium gave messages from Spirit. These messages were from loved ones who had passed away, those who had died.

A medium is someone who has learned to make that link to Spirit, to be able to bring the two worlds together, to bridge that gap. Bringing information through that you and only you, the recipient, can understand.

I was mesmerised. All these people were full of emotion as the medium brought through message after message from their deceased loved ones. It was incredible. The messages were full of love and upliftment, and you could see the light and love shining on people's faces as they received these glorious messages.

~❖~

Then I was shocked as I realised that the medium was talking to me! This was my first time in a spiritualist church, and I was being picked out. I did not want to accept his message, as it meant I would have to talk and come out of my hiding place in the back row. My fears were getting the better of me, and I was reminded of when I was at school. I always sat at the back of class, and if the teacher had to speak to me, all heads turned to look my way. I couldn't escape. And now it was happening here, too, as the medium insisted that his next message was for me.

I was very hesitant to accept that this was for me. I was frightened, trying not to be noticed but this message, the information being brought through, could only be from my beloved Nana. Of all people! She was here, trying yet again to help me, trying to let me know she was here with me.

The medium gave me information from Nana specifically about her. She talked about her dress, description, personality, everything I knew about her, even the cigarette hanging from the corner of her mouth. Then he started talking about the things that were going on in my own life right now.

I sat in stunned silence. How did the medium, know all of that? Where was all this coming from? He didn't know me; I had never been here before. It was like he was in my head, like he'd been with me in the weeks leading up to being at the church that day. It was incredible and comforting all at the same time. Nana was there, with me, watching me, knowing how I was feeling. Knowing I needed her help!

It was the most incredible feeling. I felt instantly lifted, but how? I felt a whole wave of healing come over me, but how? I felt loved, but how? How? How was all this possible?

Then the service was over. Teas and coffees were served by a really happy, rounder lady, with rosy cheeks. She was obviously in her element, standing in the church kitchen, helping and greeting everyone as they came up for their teas.

Then there was the chatter. The loud buzz of excited people talking about the medium, the messages, their church. There were the obvious friendships, too. It was warming to watch and to be a part of. It felt infectious. They all looked as if they belonged. And so too did I.

A few people came up to me to ask who I was and why I was there. I was a bit hesitant at first. What was this wonderful feeling, like coming home? But how? How could I belong? I knew no one. I felt uplifted, but I didn't know how or why. I felt motivated somehow, even though I didn't understand what was happening. What I did know for sure was that it made me feel really good. The best I had felt in a very long time.

That was the beginning of a beautiful friendship with and connection to Spirit. My initial fears and uncertainty were now gone. Spirit being around me now was different. I felt this strong feeling of love, of belonging, a warm serenity engulfing me. Spirit was working with me, not against me, and I knew this. It felt incredible.

I felt that in this beautiful, sacred space with all the new, like-minded friends I had made, I was safe. For the first time in what seemed like forever, I felt like I belonged. People liked me, and they cared about me.

This was now my sacred space. My haven! I was not frightened; I knew that I was supposed to be working with Spirit, and I knew that Spirit wanted to work with me. I knew also that they would do it in a way that was comfortable and acceptable to me. They had proved to me that they were not trying to scare me, and that this would be a partnership.

From this time, I went to the church whenever I had the opportunity. I couldn't get enough of the people or the learning. There were still many times that I would go in feeling despondent and unhappy but come out... wow. I would come out like I had the strength to fight the world and could deal with anything – absolutely anything. It was a very special time for me.

It was like a drug or a fix, if you like. It kept me going from week to week. Knowing that there was more to life than just 'this'. 'This' being pain, unhappiness, and the feeling of being unloved, unwanted, and alone.

I could not explain these new and exciting feelings, and I did not want to question them. I just knew it was helping me, and at the time I desperately needed all the help I could get.

I was happy to just accept it. I was now feeling loved, wanted, and part of something that felt very special indeed to me.

Even though the people at the church were still relative strangers, they shared with me, and this was something I had not experienced in a long time. They knew that Spirit was there, on our side and willing and able to help us in all sorts of ways. If they believed this, then I would trust that feeling and believe it, too.

I continued to go, making friends, listening to the different mediums, and getting many messages from Spirit, almost weekly. It was incredible. I was being picked on weekly, given exactly what I needed. That wonderful feeling of not being alone – that there was a whole crowd of people in Spirit who knew me and were popping in to say, 'we are here', 'we see your pain', 'we want to help you', or even just 'hello'.

But now I wanted more. I wanted to learn what this was all about. Little did I know how much of a huge impact this was to have on my life and my future. It was to be such an enormous, joyous shift for me, and this was only just the beginning.

'Evidential mediumship' is Spirit bringing information through about themselves when they were alive that you, the recipient will fully identify with.

My understanding of 'old school medium' means their training was thorough, extensive, and taught under not learned well-trained teachers from established training schools. Their messages are accurate, delivered well, compassionate and ethical. You, the recipient, are able to acknowledge all the information that is given to you.

It was obvious to me, from the evidence given to me at each service through many different mediums, that they, Spirit, were with me. They were watching over me and preparing me for something. All these mediums couldn't be making it up or be wrong. The theme of the messages was always similar, every one of them.

Messages from Spirit don't have to be life-defining moments. Sometimes just knowing that they have been around you, in your home, watching what you are up to, is enough.

This is an example of one of those messages given to me in the very early days.

One Sunday I walked into church with my daughter, Victoria, who was 2 years old. As usual I was flat, unhappy, and needy, but today I was also late and very flustered.

The medium would not have seen this, as they are always kept in a separate room until it is time for the service to begin. This room is called the mediums' room. This practice is to allow the medium to meditate if they need to or to gather their energies in preparation for working at the service.

The church was quite busy this night and there was a shortage of spare seats. However, I found a seat and sat down with my daughter on my lap. I had brought a pencil and paper for her to draw during the service as it was a long time to try to keep her occupied and quiet. This worked most of the time.

The hall was quiet as the door to the mediums' room at the side of the hall opened, and out came the chairperson and the medium. They both ascended the platform and took their seats.

The medium on this particular day was an old school, traditional medium, Ron Heron. He was dressed in a well-worn black suit and tie, with a crisp white shirt and highly polished shoes. He was an older man I had seen a few times before. He talked like a BBC television presenter, in that very British way, identifiable with early TV in England.

The service started and we had the opening prayer and a few words from the chairperson with a couple of hymns dotted throughout. Ron gave a wonderful address that was enlightening and funny. He had a great sense of humour and I loved the way he brought that into his work.

He started to deliver his messages and then talked to me. He told me this message was coming from my Grandad, who Ron described perfectly. "I have this man," he said, "he is very tall and so thin. He tells me he's your dad, but wait a minute he now says he was like a dad."

He continued, "He shows me his legs go all the way up to his chest and he is walking really fast."

We had lived with my Grandad, and he took care of us often when Mum or Dad were out. He had been a champion walker for the army, and I often commented on photos of him that his legs went straight up to his chest. *Wow. How does he know all this?*

Then Ron started laughing. "He is showing me a lipstick, but it's everywhere and I see a little girl covered in it."

He continued, "Your Grandad is telling me he was watching you before you came out tonight, and the little girl sitting with you was covered in this pink lipstick and had covered almost everything in your room with it, too."

Ron was very entertaining in the way he was describing this event and was very comically mimicking putting on lipstick. He talked as if he had been standing next to me in my bedroom before leaving for church.

Grandad told Ron that Victoria had taken one of my lipsticks out of my handbag. She had been trying to copy Mummy, but instead of just her lips had covered her whole little face. The mirror and other furniture in our bedroom were smeared with this pink lipstick also.

Ron said that the Spirit world thought it hilarious. He said that I had been incredibly worried about being late for church and had tried frantically to clean up the mess. They also knew I would have got into trouble! Her dad was due in before I got back from church, and he would have freaked out about the mess.

I sat there listening, stunned, as the medium relayed all this information with so much detail and accuracy. The colour of the lipstick, how she had taken it from my handbag. It could have been on a dresser or in a drawer, but he said, from your handbag. All these minute details, not just about the lipstick but my Grandad's description also.

His hilarious description made the whole audience fall about laughing. I too joined in the laughter with the rest of them as he very dramatically described what had happened only hours before. It was exact in every minute detail. I had known this would make me late for church. It did, I was late, I sneaked in at the very last minute and was lucky to find a seat.

How did he know? Ron had not been in my house, and so it made sense that my Grandad MUST have been there to witness all this, with the medium able to hear my Grandad talking to him and to see the pictures my Grandad conveyed to him.

These messages were wonderful proof to me that our unseen loved ones are there, watching over us. They see all the tiniest details of what we do in our everyday lives and try to help us whenever they can.

The comfort that brings to us, as it had to me this day, is immeasurable. Also, how much pleasure must the Spirit world get, to continue to share in our normal lives, enjoying the fun and laughter along with us.

It is wonderful to know that as I navigated through a very difficult time in my life, Spirit were there with me, helping and guiding me, giving me messages from the other side of life that were full of positivity, love, and compassion. I just had to learn how to pay more attention to the signs they were continually throwing at me.

What are these signs? How can I be more aware of Spirit intervention? I need to learn.

It also made me realise that no matter WHAT I faced in that period, my Spirit family were with me regardless. This gave me what I needed to get through those difficult times. More importantly, I knew I was not alone. They were there with me, helping me and proving their presence to me.

These regular messages from Spirit were the best medicine I could have received. My home situation had not changed, but the fact that my Spirit family were there changed everything. It made everything I was going through sort of bearable.

We were also lucky at the church. Each week two members of the committee would be nominated to write all messages received from the medium down on paper. This meant you could take them away and look at them afterwards.

When a medium is working with you, it can be an emotional process, and you can't always remember every detail about your loved one at the time. Some mediums can also give their information quite quickly, making it harder to grasp the full meaning.

Having these messages written down means you can look at them more carefully, understand them better, or get the information validated by other family members, if necessary. Sometimes this recognition process can take a week, a month, or even a year. Having that piece of paper means you can peruse them in your own time.

I still have those handwritten messages, and from time to time I will look through them to see what information I was given. It's wonderful to see just how much they helped me to deal with life in those days AND how accurate the mediums were.

It also shows that special connection between the Spirit world and our physical world. The closeness, the attention to detail – they are showing us they are truly with us, without a doubt.

Over the years, I have seen so many of these remarkable old-school mediums, some of whom are no longer with us, but who were very inspirational to me at the time. They gave their messages with love, compassion, sincerity, honesty, sometimes humour, and integrity.

In no time at all, I became aware of the various classes held weekly at the church. I was intrigued; my appetite had been whetted.

These classes consisted of mediumship development for beginners and advanced students, as well as speakers, and philosophy classes. I went to them all. I couldn't get enough of the church, the people, or the knowledge I was gaining. My understanding of the Spirit world was growing. At the same time, I still had that feeling of love and belonging.

As soon as I walked into the church, it felt like magic was happening; I was transported into another world. My happy, safe, sacred place.

It's funny when I look back, as at no point did I ever want to become a medium myself. I was just fascinated by it all. I had a thirst for everything spiritual. I wanted to soak up as much knowledge as I could, of everything I could access. But it was just a pure learning experience for me.

I laugh at this now as I realise that if Spirit have their eyes set on you to work with them, they will do exactly that. You just can't get away from it. I tell my own students, "Once they have their hooks into to you, they ain't going to let you go."

I also tell my students that Spirit see us like beacons of light. Some of these beacons shine brighter than others, and these are the ones Spirit know they can work with.

Spirit are constantly around us and watching. In the meantime, we may have unexplained, strange things happening, or have had certain experiences, for instance lights going on or off, feathers appearing, seeing things out of the corner of our eye, etc.

It's Spirit getting excited. I can just imagine them saying, "Woohoo, look, there's another one for us to work with, they aren't getting away from us". This is very special indeed.

The time was right, and I now had to look at learning how to do all this. I decided I would join the beginner's development group. I had no idea how to talk to dead people. How was I going to do this? Having watched several mediums give such wonderfully accurate information, I wanted to know more. I was fascinated.

How do they do this? Could I do it?

For me, this was a case of me trying to satisfy my own curiosity. I had no intention of doing this work myself. Ever!

The class I joined at the church had consisted of 15–20 people who came each month. The group was mixed ability. However, some of them had been there for a long time and were therefore fairly advanced. There were some in the group who were working mediums and came to class to get extra practice. You can never get enough practice.

It was really daunting for me. I tried really hard each month, but I just didn't get it. I listened to the instructions given by the group leader, but it did not seem to work for me. *What am I missing?*

Maybe I wasn't supposed to be in this class after all. I still had no intention of becoming a medium. Was I simply wasting my time and creating frustration for no reason?

I wish there had been clearer guidance. We were told "go to the Spirit world and see what you pick up." For someone new, this was not clear guidance.

I had too many questions. *Where IS the Spirit world? How DO I get there?*

I sat there listening intently to the instructions, but still didn't get it. Then I listened to each person as our group leader went around the room asking, "What have you got?"

Most of the responses seemed to be extremely long, drawn out, and flowery. *What am I missing? Why can't I do that?*

I would look around the room, looking for answers. There must be something, somewhere in the room. Was there something lurking in the dark corners that I was missing? But I saw nothing.

I sat there listening to all the answers the other students gave and was terrified of it being my turn to answer. *I don't have that sort of information. Where did they go to get that? Am I being stupid, missing something?*

As it came round to my turn, the fear loomed. When the group leader finally did come to me, I would just say, "I've got nothing." I didn't want to embarrass myself.

Time and persistence did eventually work, but it was a very slow process indeed.

~❖~

During the following months, I slowly made lots of new friends at the church, many of whom are still there for me today. West Wickham was a beautiful, welcoming church, and I have a lot of people there to thank for where I am today and the wonderful work I am doing.

A few of these new friends were all in the same boat. We were wanting to learn more about Spirit connection but did not know how to go forward. One Sunday, after our church meeting, five of us decided to start our own circle.

A circle is a group that meets regularly in a home or hall setting, similar to the church group. The object of the group was to learn how to connect to Spirit.

We were hoping to learn on our own. It was a fun time, but a bit hit and miss really.

We sat together every week, at the same time, no matter what. Only holidays or sickness would see us miss the group. For me personally, I was working full time and looking after three young children. I was extremely unwell, not knowing how much so at the time, and was exhausted at the end of every day. I would more often than not fall asleep in the chair.

However, at the point I was supposed to be getting ready to go to class, I would wake up and always made it on time. Spirit became my alarm clock; they did not want me to miss out.

I would always arrive on time. The other girls were usually there. We sat in our usual seats. We had been told that this was the etiquette of a circle. Same seats, same time, every week.

The lights were dimmed, I think more for effect than anything. We all linked hands; a prayer would be said to protect the circle. We invited in the Spirit, in order to work with love and for the purpose of learning to make those closer connections with Spirit.

When we had done this, we went around the group one at a time. As each of us was working, we would all direct our love and energy to the student. This would add to their own energies and help with the connections they were hoping to make.

One of our ladies was a little more advanced than the rest of us and we would always know when she was ready to talk.

She had a male Spirit that worked with her, and each time he connected to her, she had a runny nose and eyes. We called this Spirit drippy nose. We got through a lot of tissues in these sessions, either because of drippy nose or because of the feelings that were brought up for each one of us.

It could be quite emotional making those links for our fellow students; after all, these were our own family members that we were bringing through, and the tears would undoubtedly flow.

This class went on for about five years, and I made very slow progress. I also continued the classes at church and the weekly services. I was basically at the church whenever I could be.

The first group I belonged to disbanded for various reasons, so I was looking for a new group to work with. With most development circles the places are limited, and you have to be invited in. The circle leader also needs to know that you are a right fit for the group, so the selection process can be quite tough.

I put it out in the church that I was looking for a new group and waited a few months before my invitation came to join Gwen's group.

Gwen was an older member of the church. She was a wonderful healer, and her energies were just lovely.

I was happy to join her group of six. The first week I went along, and I was disappointed that I got nothing. But then the second week I went in, and I could not believe what I was saying:

"I have a man here who has an amputated leg, below the knee," I said.

One lady replied, "Yes."

I continued, "He is showing me him playing a saxophone; would you understand?"

"Yes," she replied.

And there it was – I had gone from nothing to this level of information being given to me.

This was a new group with different energies, and it obviously worked very well with me.

I do know that in my previous group that even though I didn't think I was visibly developing, Spirit had in fact been building my crushed Spirit. Spirit had now got me to the place I needed to be in order to further my mediumship development.

One week, at the Sunday service, a lovely medium called Ian Taylor was on the platform. He was very unorthodox in his way of dressing and in his way of delivering his messages.

No formal suit for Ian – he would turn up in jeans and T shirt. There was always a lot of tittering from the audience when he came in. The older members of the church especially came out with comments like "it's just not right, look at the way he's dressed." But his mediumship was superb and full of the in-depth, accurate evidence.

I was lucky that this day I was picked out by him. There was my Nana again from Dad's side of the family. She and Grandad, who had also passed by now, were both coming through on a regular basis, which continued to bring so much comfort to me.

Ian told me, "She is telling me that you will be doing this work."

"Oh, don't be so stupid, that won't be happening," I blurted out, rather loudly.

He and the audience laughed after my outburst. He was very adamant that the information he had been given by Nana was correct. The audience had seen my progress with my spiritual work and therefore knew he was right, too.

Little did I know at the time how accurate the message was to be.

Many other mediums continued to give similar messages from Spirit, telling me that I would be working with Spirit. How could that be? I certainly was not good enough at this time.

My spiritual journey continued, with me growing in strength, knowledge, and trust. Learning as much as I could about Spirit, their lives in the Spirit world, and their connections with us here in our physical world.

I devoured books and went to as many workshops, classes, training as I could. My whole world became about Spirit. Not in an unhealthy way, but in a thirsty way; I wanted to know as much as I could, everything about these Spirit connections. EVERYTHING!

I was fascinated by the stories of the pioneers of spiritualism and believe all who work with Spirit should have some knowledge of the history.

This era was a very important time for Spirit and spiritualism. These men and women paved the way for us to work with Spirit. I was horrified to learn some of the obstacles they had to overcome, and whether the Spirit communications were accepted or not.

During the 1700s there was a great need for social, health, education, economic, and working changes as well as abolition. Most people lived simple lives, with a divide of the rich and poor. Social and economic conditions were very difficult, especially for women and children. Education was mainly for the wealthy with very limited access for the lower classes. Money could get you on in life, and if you didn't have money, then your chances were extremely limited.

Robert Owen (1771–1858) was a social reformist who envisioned a better future for humanity. This was to include better living and working conditions with appropriate wages for both men and women. He also was adamant about education for all. He gained an interest in the new, up-and-coming spiritualism after befriending a medium called Mrs Maria Hayden. He had visited her to borrow a book. When they were talking, both were able to hear rappings. There was no explanation for these rappings.

She felt that this was Spirit trying to get a message through to Owen. She connected to Spirit, and there was a message for him from his parents who had passed. This message stated that he was to become a prominent pioneer of spiritualism. After his passing, and through the mediumship of Emma Hardinge Britten, who brought Owen through, he narrated the original Seven Principles to her.

This was an era in which people in general were looking for change; here were the reforms, new machinery, and changes to laws that were so necessary.

This was a time of breaking down barriers, as people began to question the basis of all religions as their churches and religious beliefs were not giving them the comfort and solace they would have normally given.

Therefore, this emergence of Spirit communication would, to a lot of people, have been the answer to the cravings for new ways, beliefs, and the help that was so desperately needed.

Spirit themselves must have felt the time was right, and they wanted us to be aware of the unseen intellectual energies that could help. This was Spirit's opportunity to show themselves to be intelligent beings who could help us when required.

Then, in the mid-1800s, along came the Fox sisters with their claims of being able to communicate with a discarnate Spirit. This was in Hydesville, USA, in 1848, where the young sisters were woken by rappings coming from one of the bedrooms in their home.

This had obviously frightened the whole family, but in time, the girls were able to work out a code. They worked out that this was the Spirit of the murdered Charles B. Rosna, a peddler who had visited the house approximately five years previously and was murdered by the then-owner Mr John Bell, who buried Rosna's body in the cellar. All this information was given from the Spirit messenger, who they nicknamed Mr Splitfoot.

This sparked much interest in the surrounding area and people came to witness these rappings for themselves, with many questions being asked of the Spirit and answers being written down. Approximately 22 statements were taken from such people. The story has changed over the years due to new documentation coming to light; however, the basic story is correct.

The Fox sisters were to travel the world, demonstrating their abilities to communicate with the Spirit world. They were challenged and tested many times by scientists, questioned by church ministers, and slated in the press. They were accused of fraud and the whole episode as a hoax.

This new phenomenon caught the interest of many prominent people, for example, doctors, scientists, teachers, ministers, and authors, amongst others, who questioned and investigated in great depth.

Many of these people went on to become spiritualists themselves. They were fortunate to have the time and money to put into investigating and championing these new spiritual occurrences. They also organised various public demonstrations of mediumship and of course the famous seances visited by many Spirits in which they could communicate with loved ones, bringing absolute proof of their existence.

This was a time for Spirit to push themselves forward, to prove to people that when our loved ones die, we have not lost them forever. They also showed us that with the right people, intent, and training, this belief would bring much comfort, joy, and upliftment to millions throughout our world, which of course it has done.

The mediums' connections to Spirit were tested beyond belief. The ridicule they went through, the strip searching before seances and other sessions. Some of the mediums were even arrested and sent to prison. A lot of their work had to be carried out behind closed doors due to the ignorance of people who simply did not understand what they were doing and instead judged them from a space of fear. People are frightened of things they do not understand, of change.

Why did these pioneers continue this work? What was their drive? I wanted to know. To feel and understand their passion for this work. This was why I studied the history of spiritualism, to get a better understanding.

I believe our forefathers went through these difficulties to make it possible for us, today, to work in our religion of spiritualism. To continue to show the world that there is no death. Our physical body dies, but the Spirit never does. We are an energy source; this cannot be destroyed. That energy survives physical death.

Thanks to these incredible pioneers, modern-day spiritualists are now able to practice our religion in comparative comfort and continue the good work they started.

I wonder if we today would have had as much strength as these pioneers. We owe them a lot.

This energy of us in the physical includes our personality, the experiences we have had in this earthly life. This energy is what a medium taps into, to bring those wonderful messages of love through from the Spirit world.

The medium makes their connection to Spirit, they listen, and then feel, see, or hear the information that is being transferred from the Spirit world.

This is known as:

Clairvoyance – clear seeing (of Spirit)

Clairaudience – clear hearing (of Spirit)

Clairsentience – clean sensing (of Spirit)

Our physical body is just the vehicle that carries the Spirit, and when our time is up on earth, the physical vehicle is no longer required, so we leave it behind.

When we have physical death, our Spirit goes home. Home to the Spirit world.

Before we came to earth, we were told of the lessons we would need to learn while here. This is part of our spiritual progression.

Every lifetime takes us further up that spiritual ladder, if you like, until our soul has learned everything we need to know.

When we go back, we will be questioned as to whether we completed the last task Spirit set us correctly and in full. What have we learned in this last lifetime? Did we learn what it was we were sent here for? Do we need to return to this physical earth again to complete that task or learn a new lesson?

The knowledge that Spirit works alongside us is still a miracle to comprehend. Those that come through with their messages don't have to be an important or famous person. For many of us, just the knowledge that our own loved ones are still around, helping, guiding, loving, and supporting us is all that is needed.

By now I had moved from the beginner's class. I had started to give fairly good information from Spirit. Some of it accurate and some not, but I had been making progress. I was then invited by the teacher to the advanced class, which was a big step. Our class teacher was Geraldine Ford, and she obviously saw that I was getting better. She suggested that the advanced class would push me more and help my progress and further development.

She was a very no-nonsense, straight-talking, purple-haired medium and teacher. I had a lot of respect for her. We always had an audience to practice on, which is vital to progress, and they were very accepting of us students.

We would be on the platform, and she would stand by the side of us and blend her energies with ours, to make sure that we were connecting to Spirit correctly and giving the information that we were being given, not what we thought it was. That is, what Spirit is telling us, not what was in our heads.

Another teacher I know says: If you are thinking, you are not linking!

Geraldine had been trained by the late, great Gordon Higginson at the Arthur Findlay College. She was brilliant to watch.

I loved Geraldine's encouragement and support, and she really did push me. She was a very likeable lady with a funny sense of humour and great personality. This helped to bring out the best in all of her students, but more importantly for myself.

I stood there on stage, with her by my side. I made my links to Spirit, and I gave my information. The next thing I knew she had blended her energies with me, and we were seeing and hearing the same things that Spirit was showing me.

In one of these classes I was standing up there and I said, "I have a ring."

Her response was, "What sort of ring? Does it have a stone? If so, what colour?"

I went back to Spirit and worked that part out. Then she asked, "Who do you have to give the ring to? Who is your recipient?"

I again was able to work that out as Spirit showed me where to go. Now I had to move on to the message, which I again was able to do. Spirit was telling me what to say; the words were in clearly in my head.

In another reading, I said, "I can see a book."

She replied, "What is the subject matter? Look at the spine of the book for the title."

She really knew how to push us to get the best out of us. On this day I was not able to get the title of the book but was proud that I was shown the subject matter. The recipient confirmed this to me.

I was really taken aback when at the end of this class she approached me.

"I'm doing a church service on Wednesday," she told me, "and I would like you to come along to do it with me."

Oh, my goodness, I gulped extremely hard.

"You only have to do one reading," she said. "I just want you to get the experience of a church platform."

I didn't dare argue with her. I agreed to meet her on Wednesday at Kingston Spiritualist Church.

The church was a purpose-built spiritualist church whose cornerstone was laid by Sir Arthur Conan Doyle, who was a great spiritualist and pioneer. More history that fascinated me.

The day of my very first demonstration came around exceedingly quickly. I drove there full of nerves and, as usual, got lost. I was in an area that I was not familiar with. I had to navigate one-way systems and traffic! I am terrible with directions, even to this day. I also had difficulty finding a parking spot. None of this was helping my nerves.

Walking into the church, I introduced myself to the church secretary. "I'm Val, I was invited by Geraldine to work with her today."

"Oh yes," said the church secretary. "Come on in while we wait for Geraldine to arrive. She did tell us you would be joining her today."

I followed her into the tearoom and sat down, and a gloriously colourful tea lady, Rosa, made me a cup of tea. She was a bubbly, bouncy, rosy sort of person with a strong foreign accent. She could see I was nervous. "I have made you an extra special cuppa," she told me. This also included some of her fruit cake, specially made for the service.

Even though I was full of nerves, the friendliness I was shown helped a little. The secretary was lovely and tried really hard to alleviate my nerves. She chatted constantly about the church and Spirit and asked me about myself. All this was certainly helping me.

I was dressed in a very smart suit; my hair and my make-up were perfect for the occasion, but the obvious nerves were shown in my uncontrollable shaking.

Time marched on, but there was still no sign of Geraldine! I kept looking towards the door every time I heard a noise, thinking it would be her. My heart was leaping all the time with the anticipation of it being her.

Another cup of tea was placed in front of me, and now I found the conversation was making me more nervous by the second.

I kept glancing at the clock, which ticked loudly on the wall in front of me. The two o'clock start time was looming.

I then heard the words I was dreading from the secretary: "You're going to have to do the service yourself."

Geraldine did not turn up. We found out later that day that her car had broken down, but there was no way of her letting the church know as these were the days of no mobile phones.

Is this Spirit working their own magic? Are they pulling strings again, changing things?

What the people at this church didn't know was, that up to that point, I had only been doing practice classes, one message at a time. I had never had to do an address, to talk, or to construct a prayer. But here I was today, and I was expected to do all these things and at least six connections to Spirit and they all had to be done WELL.

I was then ushered out of the tearoom and down a darkish corridor that led onto the main hall at the front of the church. We came out of the door, turned towards the stage, and went up three little steps on to the platform. I was shown my seat. It seemed as if this was all going on in a haze; I was that nervous I didn't know what was happening around me.

Then, as I turned and sat in my seat, there in front of me was an audience unlike any I had seen in a spiritualist church before. It was packed. PACKED to the rafters. I didn't recognise any of them but the smiling face of a gloriously excited Rosa – thankfully. She smiled reassuringly at me, bless her.

My head went into a spin at that point, my heart and head thumping so loudly I couldn't think. What was I going to do? I felt numb and sick at the same time.

The chairperson was talking away to the audience, explaining the order of service, and then to my shock and horror I heard her say, "And now, Val it's over to you!"

This was where I thought the panic would really set in. But in that instant, I was asking Spirit for help. Please stop the pounding. Stop the shaking. I want to do the best I can here today for you, Spirit, and the audience. PLEASE!

They were listening.

Then the realisation hit me, that all the eyes in that room were upon me. Looking at me expectantly. Why? Because they all wanted a message from a loved one, a mother, father, brother, lover! They were all in need. Every person in that room was expecting me to connect to their loved ones and bring that message of love and hope to them.

Then the magic really started. Those beings in the unseen stepped forward, and Val got pushed to one side. Someone or something else had control. The words that flowed from my lips were not my words. Unfamiliar phrases were spoken. My mannerisms changed. Spirit took over. They found a voice for the words of love, encouragement, pride, upliftment, and confirmation they needed to pass on to their loved one in that audience. I became animated in ways I was not familiar with. My body changed with every message I gave. One minute a lady for her husband, the next a son for his mother, then the mother for her son, and so it continued for the rest of that afternoon.

Spirit found the vehicle to do this. They were just as excited as the audience to have these 'extra five minutes to communicate their love'. The magic was now unfolding.

One of the loveliest messages I gave that night was to Rosa herself. "I have a man standing here with me who tells me he is your husband." Rosa burst into tears immediately. "I know he is short for a man, but not as short as you." She giggled and nodded in confirmation with tears streaming down her face. "He misses dancing with you," I continued, "and tells me you were the love of his life." She nodded in agreement, as she could not speak with the emotion soaring through her whole being.

"I don't want to remind you about my passing, but I could not breath, I had tubes everywhere, I was ready to go." More tears. "You were holding my hand as I passed, and you were the only one by my bedside, thank you." Poor Rosa was crying many happy tears by now. "I hear you talking to me daily; you talk about the memories and our family, and I am there with you. I still love you very much."

I should not have worried as I did it all. I worked my way through the whole service. Spirit worked with me in the most amazing way; I just had to let go and trust that they, the Spirit world, were going to work with me, and I was in the right place at the right time. And yes, there I was! I did it.

So many happy smiling faces, more acknowledgement of the information I was giving, and then at the end of the service, a huge round of applause, which is unusual in a spiritual church service. I was humbled, to say the least, and very relieved.

Afterwards, in the tearoom, I was bombarded by people telling me how good I had been and they had many questions. "How long have you been a working medium?" and "Where have you worked?" I didn't have the heart to tell them the truth that this was my first time. But boy oh boy was I thanking Spirit.

I have since thanked Geraldine a thousand times; this was after all my baptism of fire. I was meant to have been there that day on my own. Spirit had worked it all out, I know that now. I did a great job, the best I could do. The best I could do for Spirit.

When they know the time is right, they will work miracles. I certainly felt like that on this actual day. The day was successful; Spirit had made sure of that.

Spirit knew I was ready even if I didn't know it myself. They had put me in that position, as difficult as it was for me, but they didn't let me down, and I didn't let them down either.

I continued with my training in the advanced platform class at West Wickham, where there was another budding medium, David Ingman.

David had recently lost his son. He was an accountant by profession, a very logical man, and very sceptical about all this spiritual stuff. But the loss of his son started him searching for his own answers regarding the Spirit world and its true existence.

He set up a spiritual centre called the Sevenoaks Awareness Centre. With his own training, he hoped to be able to contact his son himself. Many who have lost a loved one try to do this. That's why he was at the West Wickham class.

I was shocked when he approached me one night at class and said that his medium for the following Sunday had cancelled, and asked if I would like to take the service.

Well, I can't tell you how horrified I was. I told him, "I am not capable, and definitely not ready." I suggested he ask one of the others in the class: "They are far more experienced than me."

He wasn't having any of it, insisting that Spirit had told him to ask ME!

I had already done the service for Geraldine at this point, BUT I was supposed to have shared that with someone experienced. On this occasion, however, he was asking ME to do a service on my own! That was a different kettle of fish completely!

I was really quite terrified at the thought of it and continued to argue with him that I was not ready. He was very insistent. In the end I said to him, "Why don't you leave it with me overnight and I will think about it."

I tossed and turned that night, not sure what to do. I know that I should have trusted Spirit and just asked for their help, but in my panic, I didn't think of doing that.

The following morning, I got up for work as normal, prepared myself, and went to work. I don't know what possessed me, but at 9 am I picked up the phone, called David, and said, as quickly as I could, "I don't know why I'm saying this, but yes, I'll do the service." And then I hung up the phone before I had a chance to change my mind!

The day for that Sunday service came, and again I was nervously excited. *Could I do this? Will I be good enough?*

I drove to Sevenoaks in Kent, a place I wasn't familiar with. The parking here was across a very busy road and was difficult to get to and to park in. None of this was helping my nerves.

Why can't things be easier?

The hall was small, but there was a fair-sized audience and a beautiful old lady who was sat at an electric keyboard. She was dressed so regally; she looked like the Queen.

David was a welcome face. He greeted me and introduced me to his gorgeous wife, Jean. I became very good friends with them both later.

All who were there tried to make me feel relaxed. They had been pre-warned that I was a novice and would no doubt be very nervous, and were trying to help me be at ease.

What have I let myself in for and why?

There was suddenly a silence over the room. I was introduced. The service started.

Suddenly I was catapulted once again into a full spiritual service. I did the prayers and the address. Then I was invited to do the demonstration of mediumship, connecting to loved ones from Spirit. Everyone shifted nervously in their seats as they sat and waited for my connections to be made. I stood up nervously; I began to make those links to Spirit and then, without hesitation, Spirit took over. Oh, how relieved I was.

I could not believe when a young man came through. "My wife is in the audience; I am her husband." I searched around the room and found my connection.

He continued "I had a heart attack; everyone was extremely shocked as I was an extremely fit person." The lady in the audience had silent tears rolling down her cheeks. "I was not at home when this happened, I was at work."

"Yes," she said.

He gave far more information about their family and what she had been up to since his passing, and finally added, "Oh, and thank you for the great send off and draping my coffin in my team colours."

She gasped. "We put his football colours on his coffin and all around the room."

Spirit did not let me down. They had seen another opportunity for me and ceased it. Everyone at Sevenoaks was thrilled with their messages and the way I had conducted the service. This boosted my confidence no end.

Why did I have such difficulties TRUSTING and believing that Spirit would be there, working with me and helping me always? Learning to trust was to take some time. But I shouldn't have worried; they WANTED to work with me. I just needed more practice and experience.

These two events launched me on my spiritual pathway. I was now a demonstrating medium. From this point on, I didn't look back. The bookings flowed in from other churches all over South East England. I was a medium! I was performing!

I would say to all those reading this that, if you are at the beginning of your spiritual pathway, always trust your teachers and listen to them. They would not put you forward to work with Spirit if you were not ready for it.

However, on the contrary, if they say you are NOT ready, then listen to that also, because they are the experts and know better. My teachers, both physical and spiritual, knew that I was ready, and they wanted me out there working.

Thank you! Thank you! Thank you! I will be forever grateful.

This was where I decided I needed more training, and I followed up some information I had on the Arthur Findlay College. I had heard and read about it enough, and now it was time for me to go myself.

CHAPTER 4

Progression of My Training

The Arthur Findlay College

I continued to go to any workshops or classes I could find so that I could better my mediumship and understanding of Spirit. I continued to learn from anyone I could. I wanted to do the best, and I wanted to be the best. But to be the best, I had to train with the best.

The Arthur Findlay College, the world's foremost college for the Advancement of Spiritualism and Psychic Studies, is the most spectacular place and is renowned as the best teaching facility for psychic studies in the world.

At the time I had young children and knew it would be difficult arranging my family commitments, especially as I was still going through such difficulties at home. But I put it out there to Spirit and arranged my first course. The magic was about to happen.

I had to put a lot of planning into organising the course. My family and the financial commitment had to be taken into consideration. But whatever happened, I was going! I had to!

Finding a course can be daunting due to how many there are to choose from, as well as the variety of different tutors you can select. Many of the students who go there have travelled from all over the world.

I was really excited to be sharing this week with my beautiful friend Gwen. She had been a few times previously but agreed to come with me. She had been helping me in my own development for over a year now in her personal circle, and she knew that I needed to be pushed by more experienced and qualified teachers than herself. She was excited for me that I had made this decision.

The day came for us to head to Stansted Hall in Mount Fitchet, the Arthur Findlay College.

I was excited beyond belief. *Am I really going to this famous college to further my own learning? What will this lead to?*

I felt like a kid at Christmas with the excitement of all the new and wonderful things that were to come. What I was about to learn and all the new like-minded people I would be sharing this week with. I was also a little nervous.

I picked up Gwen and we drove the two hours to the hall. The conversation was extremely animated on the way up, Gwen telling me what to expect and me full of questions. I loved Gwen very much, and that she was with me at this special time for me was truly special.

The college was originally the home of Mr James Arthur Findlay, MBE JP. He was also a former Honorary President of the SNU (Spiritual National Union). It was built in 1871, but there had been a building on that site for over 2000 years.

The site itself dates to 1215, the days of the Magna Carta. Considering all that history and the energy of all the students and teachers who have passed through the college, this energy has seeped into every part of the hall and gardens. I realised I was about to walk in the footsteps of some pretty amazing people.

On his passing to Spirit in 1964, his stately home, Stansted Hall, was gifted to the SNU for the teaching and advancement of spiritual and psychic sciences.

The whole experience for me and many thousands of others is similar. It's exquisite.

We entered via the long, winding gravel driveway, which is lined with spectacular, tall redwood trees. And then there was the hall. It was grandiose, surrounded by splendid formal gardens full of roses of every colour. Behind the hall was a glimpse of the famous tulip tree that I had read about.

There were horses in the fields, and a short distance away I could see the local church and its small graveyard, in which I found out later Arthur Findlay and his wife Gertrude are buried. It is a place where students love to walk, reading the names and engravings on the gravestones.

We collected our bags from the car. I was trying to drag myself away from the formal gardens that surrounded the hall, but it was hard as they were incredibly beautiful and regal.

Then it was time to register for our course. We approached the enormous, carved wooden front door. It felt like we were stepping into another era, back in time.

On entering the house, we were greeted by original features that had been lovingly restored. The halls were decked in the plushest of carpets and the walls adorned by enormous formal paintings. There was an elegant sweeping staircase with a polished brass handrail and Ming vases seated on each landing. There were many teaching rooms, each with their own special energy.

The hall is full of love and certainly is a treasure, and I was about to experience this for myself. Not to mention the amazing standard of teaching.

This first course was about to begin. We were in the reception area registering and being allocated our rooms. There was such hustle and bustle, so many people from all over the world, and all with that same air of anticipation. The reception ladies were run off their feet. They were bombarded by many questions from all directions, but they had the right answers for everyone who asked. They were lovely.

No matter if you were there for the first or the tenth time, that excitement would always be there.

Once we had settled into our rooms, we were to meet our tutors and find out which classes we would be in.

The course was split into three or four classes, each with a separate tutor. This depended on the numbers booked in and subjects being covered.

We assembled in the main hall, where all the tutors spoke of the upcoming week and what they had planned for us. I found out I was to be with Simone Key for Mediumship and Gwen was to be with Eamon Downey for Healing.

I think for me it was one of the hardest weeks I had experienced. There was so much to take in and learn. This included lectures and practice classes and then, at the end of the week, there would be a demonstration of mediumship put on by the students. We would not know who those students were until the day before.

The classes started at 9 am with a meditation and finished at 9 pm. Seven whole days. They were long and tiring, but I did not want them to end. I learned not only the skills of mediumship but the importance of the ethics and responsibility.

The first class started. There were about 12 students in that class. We all sat in a semi-circle as the teacher walked us through our first exercise.

I was picked to work first. This is always daunting as you don't know the level of the other students, and I was a little nervous.

I stood up and our teacher said, "Who do you have standing with you?"

"I am not sure," I said. "I can feel a male energy, but that's it."

"Well ask him to tell you who he is," she told me.

"He does look like my Grandad," I said.

She told me, "Describe your Grandad, as it will probably fit the description of someone else's Grandad in the room."

I did as she asked, and a hand popped up. "Sounds just like my Grandad."

There were indeed many other similarities to my own Grandad. I then realised that it was not my Grandad who was talking to me but the Grandad belonging to my fellow student.

This was how it went all day and all week. We were pushed to get the most from our Spirit communicators.

I was a little hesitant to put my hand up and ask questions when we were given the opportunity. My questions seemed silly and unimportant.

Slowly, as the week went on, as my confidence grew daily, I was getting better at putting my hand up and putting myself up to the front.

I was able to gain such a lot from just listening to the questions of the other students. Mostly these were the simple questions I was too frightened to ask myself. But then, when I listened to the questions from the other students, I thought, *I should have asked that question myself.*

I realised we were all wanting to know the same things, just some of us were pushier than others. This helped build my confidence; we were, at the end of the day, in the same boat. There was no competition or anyone thinking themselves better than you.

We spent all day working, sharing meals, and walking in the gardens with one another, and then after our working day had finished, we wound down in the college bar.

Then came the choosing of the students who would represent their class on the final demonstration. This decision was made by the teacher, who selected the students who showed most promise and progress throughout the week. I was very happy, albeit terrified, that I was chosen!

Nerves were on high alert now. The demonstration was in the main hall, in front of the whole college; every student who was there that week would be watching. That would mean approximately 60 students.

What if I mess up? What if I get it wrong? But I have learned it is in this situation that you must put your faith in Spirit and just get on with it, and that's what I did.

I should not have been worried. Spirit had worked with me through the week and continued through that demonstration. It was incredible. I did two messages, as instructed, both of them accepted and thoroughly understood by audience members.

Our drive home was to see us both even more excited than we were coming up to the hall. We packed up the car and headed out on the gravel driveway. Oh, my goodness, what was happening? I suddenly turned to Gwen and said, "I can't believe what I am seeing – the grass is greener, the mud is muddier, and the birds are birdier."

She just laughed. "What are you talking about?"

"Well, everything has a bigger, more colourful glow," I explained. "It's like someone has gone over everything with a paintbrush, making things brighter and more magical."

She knew what I was talking about, as she had had a similar experience her first time at the college. What had happened was our spiritual awareness had been raised; we were seeing not only more Spirit but more of the spiritual energy around all the living things that surrounded us. It was crazy but brilliant at the same time.

I continued with my classes and church practices, making visits to the hall whenever I could. My mediumship was growing and was incredible.

Many years later, when I was living in Australia, I found myself again in a difficult time of my life. I had just had a major birthday, I wasn't sure if I was going to be able to stay in Australia, and my confidence had been knocked by a relationship breakdown.

I was going to the UK to visit family, and I knew that I needed Spirit's help. *Who else could help me?*

I had organised my diary for the trip and had one week still free. I wondered if there would be any chance of a course at the Arthur Findlay College. I thought I would see what was on for that week. The chances of this at such a late stage would be very slim. I could not believe my eyes; there was a mediumship course that just happened to coincide with my free week.

I rang the college and asked if there was availability. Not only was there a course, but there was one space on that course and one accommodation room left. Unheard of, especially for this specific tutor, who was always in high demand. I didn't hesitate; I booked it there and then and looked forward to spending time once again at the college.

I was really low when I arrived. We were to have interviews with the tutors to see what class we would be put in. I told them, "I am really low in myself; I have no confidence and am questioning my mediumship skills and whether I should be doing this work at all. I need help. I need to be pushed."

They were very understanding and knew of me from previous courses, and therefore I was put in the advanced group. I knew that I would have my work cut out for me. The tutor had a reputation of being really tough, but I knew that this was what I needed.

It was indeed a very hard week. It was so hard, in fact, that out of 12 students, only four ended up completing the course. The other students had found it too tough and changed to classes with one of the other tutors.

In the last day's class, the four of us were told, one at a time, to get up on the platform and do a connection to Spirit. I did exactly that, to be told by the tutor, "That's not what I have been teaching you."

Next time round for me, again I got up and did the same, I made a connection to Spirit. I thought I was doing a great job. This time I was shouted at, "That is not what I have been teaching you."

Oh, dear, I did not know what I was doing wrong; there was no explanation, either. This type of mediumship training either makes you or breaks you, that's for sure!

My final attempt, I got up and did another connection. But before the tutor could say anything, I said, "I know I was rubbish again; I'll just get off the stage." Which I did.

I must have done something right, though, as I was chosen again for the end-of-week student demonstration.

I remember that demonstration so well. I was to do two messages.

Message #1

I made my connections to Spirit. "I have a gentleman in his 50s. He has a feather boa around his neck, and I know he's performing on stage; he's a real character. I don't feel he has been in Spirit very long."

The person who claimed him was one of the course teachers.

"He shows himself with make-up, lots of make-up and dresses," I said. "He is wearing dresses and he is laughing a lot."

"Yes," came the reply.

"He is showing me his teeth; you will understand why he is showing me his front teeth, as he has issues with his front teeth."

The tutor was laughing heartily and replied, "Yes."

"He tells me you worked together."

"Yes."

The gentleman had only passed two weeks before and the tutor had indeed worked on stage with this man, who had 'buck teeth.' He told me later that he was a dear friend and was thrilled he had come through.

Message #2

My next connection was a young lady who had cancer. "She tells me she was your best friend and says you supported her throughout her illness. She is showing herself as in her 40s, with darker hair. Her hair was important to her; it was always immaculate. She tells me she loved to party."

An American lady in the audience claimed her. "Yes," she said.

"She is showing me the film *Bridget Jones* and telling me about the scene where Bridget falls out of a black cab very drunk; she is saying that was us."

"Yes," came her reply with lots of laughter.

"She is telling me this happened in London, that you were here together in London."

"Yes," she replied.

"She is raising a glass to you now," I told her. "She's telling me it's your birthday – happy birthday."

"Yes," her reply came with both tears and laughter this time.

"Thank you. She is more than grateful for your help and kindness and the love you shared. She tells me she loves you and is constantly with you."

There was rapturous laughter in the hall at this point, with everyone enjoying the stories connected to both these messages.

In the morning at breakfast, some people who had not attended the evening demonstration were asking, "What was all the noise in the main hall last night? It was so loud."

I was grateful for the teachings that week and for being chosen to be part of the mediumship demonstration. This had given me my confidence back, and I was NOT going to walk away from my work with Spirit. Spirit had sealed that deal. I was on track again and at peak performance.

That was my turning point. Spirit had helped me through a very tough week on many levels as I knew it would be, but it was just what I needed.

I was lucky and privileged to spend many weeks at the college training with different tutors over the years.

My work has grown exponentially since that time, and I am proud of all that I do, all that I am, and that Spirit has continued to work with me on so many levels to keep me here.

I treasured my time at the Arthur Findlay College and forged many fond memories with the students I met on each visit.

As well as my learning there, I was blessed to have had other teachers outside of the AFC who had been trained by Gordon Higginson, or his proteges.

Gordon Higginson was Principal of the AFC for 14 years and President of the Spiritualist National Union (SNU) for 23 years. He was very well loved and respected in these roles as well as in his roles as a medium and teacher.

Now Spirit had to take me on a journey back home! Was this to fulfil a contract?

I feel there was so much more to my coming to Australia than I first thought. But whatever it was, this was to be a major milestone in my work with Spirit.

CHAPTER 5

Australia

I was 13 when I realised I had this passion for Australia. I did not understand it, but it was there. I had just started a new school and was given a holiday project. I had to choose any subject, and I chose Australia. We had no internet in those days, so research relied on books, mainly from the library, to look for your answers.

I had seen Grandad thumbing through an old atlas and I thought it would be a good idea to ask him if he could help. I knew he was always keen to help any of us; this would be a great plan to get him involved.

I knocked on the door to his room and he invited me in. "I have a project for school, and I wondered if you could help me, Grandad."

"What do you need, Val?" he asked.

"The subject I have chosen is Australia, and I know you have your big atlas and thought we could start there. What do you think?"

His face lit up and he could not move quick enough. He immediately went to his sideboard drawer and pulled out his precious atlas, which was very old and looked as if it was being held together with sticky tape. It was a great treasure of his and well-thumbed.

He laid it down on the table in front of us and very carefully opened it up. It had a smell that I have remembered ever since –

old books, that musty smell. I still to this day love that smell, and it reminds me of my Grandad.

"Let's see what we can find, shall we?" he said, and he began gently turning the pages searching for anything to do with Australia. I was enthralled by all the beautiful pictures, of the many colourful landscapes. The strange looking animals, unusual plants, and trees. It was fascinating to me.

Together we scanned the pages for information that could be useful for me. There were vast amounts of knowledge in the pages. He found a paragraph about the fruits that they exported around the world.

"Your mum always has lots of tins of fruit," he said. "I bet if you look in the cupboards, you will find some, and you can use the labels."

I went straight away into the kitchen and rummaged through the cupboards, finding, as Grandad had said, quite a few of these tins; all had come from Australia.

I carefully removed the labels so I could add them to my project folder. I excitedly ran back to Grandad, who had been waiting patiently, and proudly showed him my find. Then, together, we went through other bits from those pages that I could use. We chatted, I wrote, he pointed things out. Such a special memory with Grandad.

My project was good; there were pages and pages, and I got the top grade for it. Both Grandad and I were extremely happy.

Mum was really cross with me when she discovered these stripped tins. We never knew what she would be opening. Oops!

Two of my aunts and uncles had already moved to Australia by this time. When I was around 16, my family were supposed to emigrate too, to join them. The family was full of how wonderful life was there, the better living, climate, and the job opportunities. After hearing all these wonderful stories, Mum and Dad were keen to move there, too. Sadly, life in the land down under was not to be, as one of my sisters failed her medical. We were all devastated by this news.

~❖~

I came to Australia for the first time for my 40th birthday, when Mum, my daughter, and I arrived for a five-week holiday.

I had planned and saved. Got our visas and tickets. Bought new outfits and was super excited. This was Australia and we were going to stay with family. They were just as excited and had made many plans of places to go and things to do and who would be having us and when.

It was the strangest thing; when we landed, I felt as if I had come home. I could not understand the feeling I had at the time, but how could that be when I had never been here before?

Many years later, I would understand this fascination for Australia and where I think it had come from. I will talk about this later.

The holiday was incredible. We travelled through Melbourne, Brisbane, and across to South Australia. The family made us feel incredibly welcome, and there were plenty of birthday celebrations for me, Mum, and one of my cousins.

When we left, I felt lost. This land down under was where I needed to be. I felt loved and wanted. But how was I going to get there?

I came back from Australia, and the reality of my home life hit me hard. I needed to get out of my unhappy marriage. Then, one day in the midst of my distraught state, I was standing alone in my kitchen; there was no one else in the house.

Suddenly, I heard Spirit voices in my head. These voices were unusually loud and remarkably insistent; I could not avoid paying attention to them. They shouted at me, "We want you to give up your business, give up your home, give up your country, and MOVE TO AUSTRALIA TO TEACH." It was that loud and that persistent.

I slowly took in what was happening and screamed back at them.

"What are you asking of me? How is this possibly going to happen? I have no money, no work to get that money. I am too old. I have nothing to offer Australia, no skills, or qualifications. It's simply not possible."

Hot tears streamed down my face, and I felt crushed. I punched the air with clenched fists as I shouted at them. Everything felt like it had turned against me, and I didn't know why.

I have always been a very grounded person as far as Spirit is concerned. There are many who lead their lives by what Spirit says, but they are here to guide us, not to live our lives for us.

I had been seeing Spirit since I was 7 and working with them since the 1990s, but my real journey with them was about to start.

I had been working very successfully in the UK up until this point. I had a day job, a secretarial services business, that I had been running for many years. I was also developing my mediumship skills.

Then, out of the blue, all hell let loose. I lost my main business. I had never been in such a dismal situation. It was Christmas 2008 and I had only £1 in my purse. I couldn't go anywhere or do anything. Everything was on the line – my home, my work and my kids' schooling. I was beside myself, not knowing where to turn or what to do.

I felt as if everything was against me, and all was lost. Not a great situation to be in, that's for sure.

I knew from my family's experiences of emigrating to Australia that the restrictions were extremely strict. This move for me was not going to be possible. *What am I going to do? I need a miracle.*

Funny how life plays out and you don't realise the significance until much later.

It just so happened that a few months before I heard these voices in my head, a friend had loaned me a book called *The Secret*, by Rhonda Byrne. I read this book twice. The first time it was a bit of a half-hearted attempt; I was busy and not paying attention to what I was reading.

However, I then read it again AND watched the movie AND played the CDs of the book constantly in my car while driving to and from work. I suddenly felt that there was an incredible message within these words. It was speaking to me. I realised that there was sense in the author's words. I needed to pay attention and do something about it.

There was such knowledge contained in this little book, but for me one of the biggest things was that it talked about the power of positive thinking and manifestation.

I had heard of this before but never practiced it myself. This was the time I had to give it a try. The book was talking to me, and I felt compelled to give this a go. I needed to move forward, and this looked like it could be the way to do it.

The friend who gave me the book said that he too had been in a bad place. He decided that it wouldn't do any harm to just change his beliefs as though the law of attraction was real and practice it for one year. This is what I did. I made vision boards, I spoke positively, I made plans as if I had a bank full of money and believed that I was living my best life.

Regarding going to Australia, this was part of this plan too. All the way through this process I was talking to Spirit and asking for their help and guidance. They had told me to go and needed their help to make this happen.

I decided to choose a date for Australia. I drew a line across every page in November 2009 and wrote AUSTRALIA very clearly across those pages.

I decided to sit back, get on with life and see what happened. That didn't mean that I was totally inactive, expecting it all to fall in my lap – not at all.

On the contrary, I imagined myself on a plane going to Australia. Every plane I saw in the sky, I would acknowledge that I was on it. I spoke to my family down under and told them of my plans. By doing this, I had made it real. I had made a promise to the family and myself, and I had to be there. I did research into my work options there, too.

Could I work? Could I get a visa? How would this work?

Christmas came and went, as did the following five months.

Then, in June 2010, out of the blue I received an email from my now very good friend Jeff, in Australia. His email was very short; all it said was, "I am coming to the UK."

I was very shocked to get this from him because I had been given Jeff's details about seven years earlier. Tim, another Aussie who I met at a spiritualist church in the UK, had given me Jeff's details. Tim had watched me work at the church and came up to me and chatted afterward.

He told me I should email Jeff; they were good friends and both into the spiritual scene in Queensland. "Tell him Tim has given you his details," he told me, "and that I have seen your work and suggest you go to work in Australia." Is there a chance he could help me?

I listened to Tim, sent off the email but I didn't get a reply. Jeff totally ignored my email! We laugh about this now.

Now there was this email from Jeff saying he was coming to the UK. You can imagine my absolute surprise and excitement to receive this email.

I replied to him immediately and asked, "What airport are you coming in to? When are you arriving? I will pick you up and you can come and stay with me!"

This was much to the horror of my children, who objected, saying, "But you don't know this man..." and "What are you doing?" But it felt right; I was being guided by Spirit.

I realise now that if he had responded to me seven years earlier, it would not have been possible for me to go to Australia. My daughter would have only been 12 and the timing would have been wrong on many levels.

Jeff responded with details of his flight, and I arranged to pick him up from Gatwick airport. He stayed with me for three nights of his three week trip.

Coincidently, I was working on those nights, and he was keen to see me work. I was doing a mediumship demonstration in two local theatres and a ghost investigation. He came to them all.

The night before he was due to travel back to Australia, we were chatting and he said, "You need to come to Australia. You work exactly like my friend Bill Harrison who has passed."

He continued, "In fact, you are the female version of Bill."

Bill was a very good friend of Jeff's who had passed away not long before, which had saddened Jeff deeply.

We talked about what had spurred me on to make the decision to come to Australia. I explained to him about reading *The Secret* and the manifestation and that I had already put the dates in my diary for November 2009. He listened intently and sat quietly for a moment.

"That's no good, mate," he said, "everyone is arranging holidays at that time of the year. Let's book it in for February 2010 and make it six weeks." Which we did.

Oh, wow, this was exciting; now all I needed was to get the money. I put it out to Spirit again that I needed the money to pay for this trip.

I was going to manifest this all. I was going to make it happen, and I wanted Spirit and the universal energies to be listening to me as well.

I made the changes in my diary. I erased all the information for November 2009 and transferred it to February 2010.

I put out to Spirit and the universe the need for money to make this trip happen. And hey presto, it all materialised. Suddenly the work, my readings, started to flow in. I also secured myself a secretarial position in London that added to the pot. This was all looking like it could happen after all.

I saved hard, I bought new clothes, and I prepared for my trip. My boss in London asked if I would like him to hold back half my money each week. His plan was to give me this money just before I was to go on my trip. Everything was working in my favour.

Jeff and I emailed back and forth to one another, the details of the work that I would do and where. This work load was growing by the day. This was all rather exciting.

What a trip that was. I was met at Brisbane airport by Jeff and his partner. I was to get a couple of days of rest with a few sightseeing trips thrown in for good measure, and then the work would begin.

This, for me, was never like work. It was like a dream come true. This work had become my life, and I was and still am extremely passionate about what I do. Anything to do with spiritual work made me happy and exhilarated.

While I was in Brisbane and in between work, I got on the phone and arranged other work for myself in Sydney. I did not know anyone in this area at all however I made calls to all the spiritual shops explaining who I was and what I did to see if I could generate any interest. I was looking for work. One of the spiritual shops in Sydney was very forthcoming and excited that I had contacted them. I ended up working with them for quite some time on that trip and on many return visits.

Likewise, I tried Melbourne. I do have quite a lot of family in Australia who are mainly based in Melbourne. Luckily, I got to visit them while I was there. I managed to secure a fair amount of work there, too, which included readings and a few mediumship shows.

All these events were well attended. Workshops up to 50 people at a time. Reading days booked out. Shows to full capacity. It was crazily busy. I was loving every moment of it and all the incredible people I was meeting.

What I found funny when I first went to Australia was the terminology being so different. Hearing words meaning such different things to the UK version of the same words.

I got it wrong on many occasions and ended up with audiences laughing at me. When they explained why nine times out of ten I felt so embarrassed.

The last part of my six-week trip was spent in New Zealand. Jeff, who was originally from there, organised an awesome amount of work for me. Workshops were again sold out, as were shows and readings at some of the spiritualist churches.

We had an incredible time visiting the most picturesque sites throughout New Zealand's North Island. It was breathtaking; I had never seen anything like it. And the people there were so humble and hospitable. "Do you need a bed? Come and stay with us."

One such family I stayed with was a Māori family with four children. They were not rich; you could see that. However, I was fed and treated like a queen. I will never forget their hospitality.

I worked within the spiritual churches there and made many new friends. It was incredible, and I really felt at home with the beautiful people in both Australia and New Zealand; they were all welcoming and friendly.

Initially, my plan was to travel to Australia for three months at a time on a business visa. At the time, my thinking that there was no way I would be able to stay for longer or even for that matter to stay permanently.

Then a chance invitation came from my friend Alex in Melbourne that was to change my life.

She had seen a notification of a talk to be held in a Melbourne suburb. The speaker was the editor of a new magazine. We both went along and listened intently to what he was talking about. The magazine had a spiritual theme, and I needed to speak to him. I felt Spirit drawing me in.

At the end of the talk, people hovered around him to speak to him. I managed to talk to him, I quickly told him who I was and what I did, and we arranged to meet over a coffee.

When we met, I told him more about myself and my dream for Australia. It was a long, animated meeting with plenty of excitement from both sides. The CEO offered me a position as a speaker for his company, which was a new magazine that had been launched not long before. The name of this magazine was *Veritas*. He also mentioned the chance of a 457 working visa.

I did not understand the significance of this visa at the time, but the excitement that he brought to the table made me think that coming to Australia permanently could happen.

We spent many hours talking with his accountants and immigration agents. A proposal was put together clarifying what work I would be doing. An application for the 457 visa was submitted. It was a very exciting time indeed and certainly not what I was expecting.

I could not believe my incredible luck or that I even had half a chance of being able to stay in Australia. It was like a dream come true. The only difficulty at the time was the cost of the visa application and the legal costs that I had to cover.

My hopes were soon dashed when the Immigration Department refused my application on a technicality, and I was given 28 days to leave the country. Papers were quickly drawn up to appeal this decision. The lawyers were not convinced this appeal was going to work, but it did buy me some extra time and cost me an incredible amount of money.

Along my travels I met a man, who was initially wonderful and so we entered into a partnership visa. After two years however I realised that this relationship was not going to work for many reasons. I got in touch with immigration and told them as much. Again, I was told I had 28 days to leave the country.

This really was another difficult and emotional time for me. I had to give up on my dream of living in Australia. I sadly started selling all the possessions I had accumulated.

Am I meant to be going back to the UK? Did Spirit not tell me I had to be here?

I did a lot of shouting at Spirit throughout this period.

A few days later, I was booked to do a day of readings with a lovely lady at her home. When I arrived, I was extremely flat. She knew this was not me and asked, "What's up?"

I explained what had happened in the last few days. She suddenly turned and went into the next room. When she came back out, she handed me a piece of paper and said, "Ring this number."

"What?"

"I know this man can help you," she said.

I said to her, "There is no one who can help me now, I have come to the end of the road. I've tried everything possible and will have to go back to the UK."

She suddenly snapped at me. "You cannot give up so easily on this opportunity. My son was in a very similar situation as you, but with his girlfriend. He was given the number of this immigration agent and they have moved mountains for him. He made this happen and they got their residency and subsequently citizenship." She added insistently, "Ring him now."

She stood there and watched as I made the call.

I rang the number and a really lovely man on the other end of the phone listened to my story. And then, I couldn't believe what I was hearing. He said, "I want you to come and see me tomorrow. Bring whatever papers you have regarding your immigration."

It turned out he was a specialist immigration lawyer and said he could help me. He added "...and I never lose a case."

The following day I turned up at his offices, shaking like a leaf, I was so scared. My visa situation had been up and down for such a long time, and I couldn't see that this man could do anything more for me. Of course, this was going to be more money.

I really thought I had come to the end of the line with trying to stay in Australia. This all looked futile. I didn't want to go back to the UK. My Australian dream was about to come to an abrupt end, and I didn't know what to do.

I wanted this man to be able to help me but as I already had one failed visa application and the relationship had failed, how could he help me? I didn't want to pin all my hopes on this man to be crushed yet again.

I sat there quietly as he went through all the paperwork. He was busily writing and filling out various forms. Then he said, "We can do this." My heart was in my mouth at this stage. *Can he? Am I hearing him correctly? Could I stay?*

The papers were emailed immediately to the Immigration Department, and all I could do now was to wait. This process was going to take some time. In the meantime, the agent told me confidently, "Go and get on with your life. It's going to be okay."

Then the news came. My application had failed! My lawyer was stunned. "How could this have happened? This was a cut and dry case." He was so shocked. He told me, "I think someone in Melbourne immigration office really does NOT want you here."

The process for an appeal was started. Again, more papers, more meetings, and as you can imagine, more money! This whole process had cost me thousands. I had a little money from earnings, but it was nowhere near enough. I was very lucky that family and friends helped me, as they wanted me here as much as I wanted to be here.

After many months, we got an appeal date. More money. I had to attend the immigration offices in Melbourne with my lawyer. It was a cold and damp Melbourne morning. We were both very sombre going into this meeting, not knowing what the outcome would be, and I suppose scared too that this would be the end of the road on my journey in Australia. I could feel the nerves pulsing through my entire body.

I asked for all the help I could get from the Spirit world, but my nerves were not helping my sense of foreboding. My lovely lawyer was likewise helping with the prayers to Spirit. He knew and believed in my work, and it became apparent that he too was of similar belief. This was wonderful for me to know.

We were ushered into a small room and given instructions by a young man as to how to address the magistrate. It was all extremely formal, very clinical, and scary. I was not allowed to speak at all. All communication was through my lawyer. If I was addressed directly, I had to address the magistrate as Madam. The nerves were certainly building by this time. I felt like I was teetering on the edge of a precipice. Everything in my life now hinged upon this meeting and her decision.

The magistrate entered; she was beautiful to look at and immaculately dressed. She was sniffling, tissues in hand; we could see that she was not well, and her attitude was one of 'do not mess with me today.'

The rules were that all our paperwork had to be submitted at least ten days prior to this meeting. I was not aware of this. I had managed to get copies of text messages from my phone the day before our meeting so I hoped these would act as further evidence to help my case.

As the meeting progressed, I put the papers on the table in front of her. From the tone of her voice, you could tell she was NOT happy. In fact, she was really angry that these papers were being given to her today! She spoke to my lawyer and would not look at me.

She finally did look at the papers, but then she pushed them back at me, saying, "I can't deal with these as they are in no specific order."

I quickly said, "I can do that now," and grabbed the papers. I was so flustered but rushed through the papers, sorting them out before handing them back to her.

At this point the tension in that room was so high it was palpable. The magistrate was not happy or well; I was flustered, nervous, and scared, and I could feel the apprehension from my lawyer also.

I kept remembering my lawyer's words; he had promised me he could make this happen, and he did not want to let me down. He had told me, "I have never failed in an application of this kind, and I will not fail you." But here we stood, neither of us sure what the outcome of today was going to be.

Then in the blink of an eye, that heavy energy changed. *What just happened?* It was so intense; you could physically feel the change. My lawyer and I could both feel it. We were sat that close to one another at this point, in this tiny room that felt like a cell. I felt him gently nudge my arm. He was acknowledging that he had felt the changes, too.

This whole thing was beginning to feel very unreal. Then, this lady who had initially looked incredibly stern suddenly warmed to us. She was smiling; her whole body energy had changed and relaxed. Then she spoke to us both, saying, "Well, I don't see why we can't provide you with this visa, as far as I am concerned; I am going to overrule this previous judgement."

What HAS just happened? I was holding my breath, almost frightened to breathe again. *Did I hear her right? She could still change her mind.* I wanted to run out of the room before that could happen.

But all the papers were finalised there and then before we left her office. It felt as though this had all happened in a flash. We said our goodbyes and thanked her, and we left the room. We were both so relieved. I am sure we both ran out of that building.

We stood outside on a very cold, damp morning in Melbourne. My lawyer and I looked at each other and said at the same time, "What just happened in there?"

I said to him, "Did you feel that whole energy shift?"

"Yes, I certainly did," he replied.

There it was – I had at last been granted my permanent residency. All that was left now was to await the official paperwork. I was staying in Australia; I was home, and this was really happening.

My dreams had come true. All those years before, Spirit had told me I had to be here; they were right. It had, however been a long, very painful process and must have aged me at least 20 years. At this point I didn't care – I could now get on with my life.

This was the happiest I had ever been, and yes, I had come home. This next story explains why I felt like I had come home.

~❖~

While I was living in North East Victoria, I set up a spiritualist church. When I first mentioned to some of the locals that I wanted to do this, I was told it would not be successful.

"It will never work," several people uttered in judgement.

How wrong were they. I found a hall, which was the local CWA hall. I created a Facebook page and started promoting it. It was going to be once a month on a Thursday evening.

Finding mediums to fill the monthly slots turned out to be a bit difficult as the towns here were miles apart. However, I managed to do this, and if I didn't have a medium, I did the service myself.

The attendance was great, with around 30 people per month. I also set up a lending library with my own books and others that had been donated to the church.

I have since left the area, but the church is still running to this day, having been taken over by a wonderful spiritual lady who is doing a great job.

While I was in North East Victoria, I realised people in country towns did not have access to events similar to the big cities. I was also aware that due to the distance between villages and towns, the people were not aware of services they had on their doorstep. I decided to do a festival showcasing not only spiritual businesses but also all the businesses in the surrounding areas.

I wanted this to be a two-day event. It was to have stalls, entertainment, and workshops and to appeal to all types of people.

I had learned from previous events I had attended in Australia that I needed to be mindful of Aboriginal culture and have a 'Welcome to Country' performed. This is a ceremony carried out by an Aboriginal Elder to acknowledge and give consent to events taking place on their traditional lands.

I rang the local Aboriginal Society and explained to them what I wanted to do. They gave me the name of a lady called Aunty Betty.

I rang and introduced myself to her and told her why I was calling. She sounded quite abrupt. She told me I would have to come to her home to meet her and discuss this. We arranged a date for me to come around.

The day came, and I walked up her front path a little nervously. I knocked at her door. The door was opened by a beautiful lady with dark, curly hair. She was around my age – in her fifties. She didn't look scary, even though she had sounded like that on the phone initially.

She invited me in. "Take off your shoes and coat!" I promptly did. I could not believe we were both standing there in identical clothes and colours, pink tops and black trousers.

She acknowledged that too, by looking me up and down and raising her eyebrows, but didn't speak.

She then told me to sit down, still in her abrupt way. She asked if I would like a drink. "I would love a cup of tea," I said, and then she walked into her kitchen. She continued to chat to me while she made the tea.

Her home was very humble and full of various Aboriginal artefacts. It turned out that she was a beautifully warm lady, and underneath that harsh exterior she had a very warm heart.

The tea was made, and she brought it out on a tray with a plate of biscuits. She then sat down and made herself comfortable.

I explained to her why I wanted to speak to her, but I feel initially she was sussing me out, trying to figure out my motives. She was not going to make a decision right then, that was for sure.

Then she started to talk to me. She told me she was part of the Stolen Generation, and my heart hurt for her. I had by that time read some books on Aboriginal history.

There were many coincidences I was seeing as we talked: places I had been to, people we knew and even our own names – my name being Hood, and hers Cherry-Hood.

I talked about some of the experiences I had had in Australia. For instance seeing the Spirits of Aboriginal men lining the road to welcome us in certain areas. The feelings in other places of being watched. This land is full of Spirit activity. I enjoyed telling her of my experiences, and she listened with much interest.

She suddenly said to me, "Spirit told me you were coming," she said. "Three months ago, I was told a Barbie Doll would walk up my front path." How hilarious was that and the fact that today I had turned up in pink with curly blonde hair?

We were sitting, chatting, sharing stories of our lives and experiences. It seemed like we had been chatting for a long time when suddenly I felt my energies change and I burst out with, "Oh, oh, oh!"

"What's the matter?" she asked, with a knowing smile.

I said, "I feel like I drifted off, almost like I was daydreaming. I could hear you talking to me, but I was transported to a different place, back in time. You were talking to me but not in the present, in this room. I was a little girl around the age of 5. I was sitting on a tree stump surrounded by bush. I had no shoes on; I could see my feet and my legs swinging. My feet didn't reach the ground. I had tatty clothes on, and YOU were my mother, talking to me. You were my Mum!"

She giggled very impishly and said, "Well, I know that." This was all she would say.

This was incredible for me! This lady who I was meeting for the first time was my mother in a previous lifetime. This was something I could not comprehend. I understood about reincarnation with my spiritual teaching, but this was uncanny.

Reincarnation is where your soul, which is immortal, can transmigrate upon death to a new infant to live again. This is all part of our spiritual progression. We have lessons we have to learn to make our Spirit pure. At this point, it is said that we will no longer need to reincarnate.

She asked me, "Where do my people come from in Australia?"

I replied, "I don't know." *How am I supposed to know that? This is all a bit much to take in, and I have no idea!*

She rang me daily for the next few days asking, "Please tell me where DID we come from?"

On about day five, I rang her. I said, "I'm standing in front of my map of Australia, looking at Uluru." I was pointing at my map with my finger hovering over Uluru.

"Yes," she said, "and now where?"

I allowed my finger to be guided by Spirit. "I am going to the right and now down a little bit."

"What is the name of the place you have stopped at?" she asked.

When I told her, she squealed delightedly down the phone, "That's where my people came from!"

It was such a wonderful experience to find this woman was with me in a past life, and she was my mother at that.

We became firm friends after this.

This was why I felt like I had come home, that first time I arrived in Australia. Here it was, my answer. I had most definitely been here before in a previous lifetime, and Aunty Betty confirmed that for me.

I was extremely happy to find this out.

Australia is my new AND my old home.

How wonderful to know this. I feel very blessed.

Coming back to the festival – it could not have gone better. It was two full days of fun, colour, joy, and love with beautiful stalls that showcased what was on our doorstep. Exactly as I had planned.

Aunty Betty spoke the Welcome to Country, and we had Aboriginal dancers and even a local Native American dancer, who performed a celebratory dance with beautiful singing. Everyone involved was all brightly dressed in their native colours. It was a spectacular vision.

There were, in all, five stage performances and two marquees with workshops taking place throughout the two days.

I approached the local Rotary club, who helped with the door, collecting money, and much more. Local businesses donated small items that went into goody bags that everyone took home with them. I was very proud of the whole weekend.

All who came to the event thoroughly enjoyed themselves. There were over 800 people who came through on the first day. It was truly a success – hard work – but I loved every minute of it.

CHAPTER 6

Is There Anybody There?

As I have been seeing Spirit since I was 7 years old, this connection/communication has become part of my normal life. For me it's like brushing my teeth every day; it's the most natural thing in the world. I get them popping in and out, letting me know they are around, letting me know when things are not right or that someone I know needs help or healing.

For many others out there, the idea of seeing dead people, or having things go bump in the night, is a very scary experience, as it was for me, too, initially.

It is wonderful however to realise that there are many people out there who do have Spirit around them but sometimes they are just not aware of the signs. These signs could be something simple. For instance, do you see things out of the corner of your eye, or does someone seem to walk past you but nobody is there?

Do you feel changes in energy, a change in temperature, or are you suddenly covered in goosebumps?

Do you just know that something is going to happen?

Do unexplained things move around your home?

You know that you put your glasses on the table, but they disappear only to be found on the bathroom floor!

There are many ways that Spirit try to let you know they are around.

Does a song keep playing that reminds you of a loved one?

Does the volume go up or down on your radio or TV?

Would that programme you keep thinking about have been your mum's favourite?

Do you keep finding feathers?

Do certain birds keep appearing or tapping on your window?

Do you get certain smells that remind you of your Mum?

Are your emotions all over the place today? What is the significance of the date?

Why do these things keep happening? It could be your loved one saying, "Hello, I am still here," or "I am aware that you are feeling low today," or "I can still help you; please let me."

I love that Spirit shows me when they are around, and personally, I have had many ways of them doing this. But sometimes it's the simplest of things that are the most pronounced.

Try looking back over your last week. Can you see anything that could have been a sign?

One day, when I was still in the UK and feeling in a state of limbo between the UK and Australia, I was a bit disgruntled with life and feeling that Spirit were not working with me as I thought they should be. I needed fresh air. I needed to clear my head and decided to go out for a walk. It was a glorious day and I felt I should not miss the opportunity.

When I am not happy with Spirit, I tend to shout at them. I work really hard for them and feel it is a two-way path and that Spirit should work hard for me, too.

As I was getting ready this day, I was shouting at Spirit, saying, "*I needed some clear direction. What am I supposed to be doing? I would really like you to give me a sign that you are still here with me.*" I had previously asked for signs and on occasion been given a feather.

That day I again asked for feathers. I set out on my walk wearing trainers and shorts, water and food in my backpack. I was not a happy bunny at all; I wanted change, I needed change, but I didn't know what or how.

I planned my route and was enjoying walking in the warm sunshine. I spoke to a few people who passed the time of day with me and bumped into a neighbour who wanted to stop for a chat. I felt a bit rude as I was not in the mood to chat; I was on a mission to get some answers from Spirit. I had to commune with them only.

I had not gone far before there, on the ground in front of me, was a feather. *Okay, one feather, so what?* Walking past the busy train station, there was another and yet another. I eventually counted six feathers. My mood picked up and I was feeling a little happier that maybe Spirit were with me and were really listening to me. Was I really convinced though?

My route then took me around a corner and under a railway bridge and there on the ground in front of me were hundreds of feathers. I laughed out loud, and I heard a voice in my head: *We have not and will never let you down.*

Obviously, a bird had been attacked by a cat or something, leaving all these feathers strewn across the path and road. What were the chances of this happening today; especially on the day when I was specifically asking for this sign. Here they were. Spirit can be funny sometimes, and I love that.

I felt more contented having seen these feathers and heard Spirit's adamant message in my head. I strode off much happier and stronger. I did not feel crushed as I had been feeling at the beginning of my day. Spirit were with me, listening to me.

I had the most exhilarating walk and felt remarkably better in myself. I knew Spirit were there, and even though I was still not clear on where or what I was going to do, it did not seem to matter.

Spirit knew what was going to happen. I was in the right place at the right time. I had to learn patience and to trust that Spirit was working with me no matter what, and that there was a purpose to all of this. I just didn't see it yet but that was okay. Maybe I wasn't supposed to see that bit just yet.

I have had much guidance over the years from Spirit but from time to time I still have doubt. I am human, after all, and we are entitled to question. I do know at the end of the day that I have had too many confirmed instances of Spirit working with and helping me to know Spirit and my loved ones will not let me down.

Initially, as a child, I found seeing dead people very scary, only because I didn't understand. I had many questions. *Who can I talk to? What is happening? Why am I seeing these dead people? What does it all mean?*

My thoughts contained other questions, too. *Am I normal? Am I going mad?* These questions always haunted me. At the time, I had no idea where to get these answers. Dealing with this on your own is the worst part.

I would like you to know that if any of this resonates with you, you are certainly not on your own. There are many places to go to talk to others about all things spiritual. Me included!

Over the years, I became aware of many like-minded people and groups where we can share our knowledge and experiences openly.

After doing this work for a number of years, I thought, maybe naively, that perhaps I could work with other religions, and we could join together in helping people dealing with death and grief. This was my first approach to a mainstream religious church.

After many years working as a medium and teacher of mediumship, I have had many clients who talked about their grief. They felt that more should be coming from their traditional churches, and I agree. I had thought about this for some time and felt it would be a great idea to speak to other religious bodies to see if we could work together to help the parishioners in their grief.

Around the corner from my home was a rather large Church of England church. I found the telephone number and rang to make an appointment, briefly explaining the reason for my visit.

I must admit it was with much trepidation that I went along to the church for this meeting. I was met by the minister and his assistant, and after the pleasantries, I explained in detail why I was there and what I was hoping we could achieve together.

My question to them: Is there a way that both our religions could work together to help people when they lose a loved one?

I told them of my readings, how I made those wonderful connections to Spirit and how that had helped a large amount of people. They knew then that their loved one was at peace and still around them.

I wanted the minister to understand how people responded to a reading and the happiness, comfort, and upliftment it brought them.

They both listened very intently to what I had to say, not responding in any way.

I finished up with, "Surely we could work together?"

There was a heavy, uncomfortable silence when I finished. They both fidgeted in their seats and rustled papers nervously.

After what seemed like an absolute age, the minister suddenly began to talk, calmly and precisely. I was incredibly shocked to hear him say, "I know why you have come to me today; you have come in order that I can save your soul."

He told me what I did was the devil's work and not the work of God.

I was stunned by what I was hearing. At that point, I realised I was wasting my time talking to them; they did not want to understand my work or entertain our working together. I switched off. There was no way he agreed with or believed in what I was doing as a spiritualist. His way was the only way, and as he had already stated, "You are doing the devil's work!"

I left very quickly and never went back, nor did I ever suggest similar elsewhere. Very sad and short sighted that this is still the case today.

Before my spiritual work took over my life, I was running another, totally different business. This was a secretarial agency where I would take in typing work. This was for both regular clients and those who walked in off the street. Over time, these clients became firm friends, and this was an experience with one such lady.

When I was working in my day job, I was in my 40's, and I met a lovely lady. She initially came into my office to get some quotes typed up for her husband's business. We became friends, sharing coffee and meals both at our homes and out and about. We grew quite close over the many months we knew each other.

I had talked to her on numerous occasions about my spiritual beliefs and my training. She seemed to be genuinely interested and regularly asked me lots of questions. It was lovely for me to find a friend outside of the church who was really interested in what I did.

One day over coffee she told me of a spiritual group that she belonged to that was holding regular gatherings, and asked if I would like to come along to one of their meetings. I said that I was interested and would love to join her.

From what she had told me, her group sounded very similar to my own beliefs, and so I felt it would be great to meet new people. I was quite excited and keen to go along.

She told me when their next meeting was planned and asked if I was free to join her on that evening. After checking my diary, I told her I would love to go. She arranged to pick me up along with two other ladies who I had not met yet. They all seemed quite nice and we chatted very comfortably in the car on the way.

It was a very long drive from our pickup point, and we seemed to be going further and further into the countryside. I had no idea where we were going as I had not been given the address, and I didn't ask, either. Eventually we arrived at our destination, and it appeared as if we were in the middle of nowhere!

We all walked up to the house, which was very large and palatial, standing in its own grounds. We knocked on the door and, on entry, were met by lovely people who knew my friend and the other two who had come with us. I was introduced to them and they all made me feel very welcome. There seemed to be quite a lot of other people in the house. All appeared fine on the outside.

After all the pleasantries, we were all ushered into a room and all the doors were locked. It was a large room where every seat was taken. Apart from my friend and the two ladies who travelled with us, none of the others looked familiar. I started to feel a little unnerved; something didn't feel right but I couldn't put my finger on what it was. The panic began to rise in my body and I was beginning to get quite scared. *What on earth is happening here?*

We were invited to sit down and join the rest of the crowd. Then, before I knew it, I was being bombarded by questions, all aimed at me! It appeared that I was the only new person in the room.

"We hear that you connect to Spirit..."

"How does that work?"

"What do they do?"

"Do you hear voices?"

"Can you see them?"

The questions were being fired at me from every direction. At first, I was only too happy to share the stories of my experiences with Spirit, which I was very proud of. I told them that I had been seeing Spirit since I was a child. I excitedly said that I had been seeing my Nana from a very young age and how wonderful it was that she helped and guided me throughout my life right up to the present time.

I had absolutely no idea what was about to happen next.

Somebody came and took me by the arm and moved me to a seat in the corner of the room; this was beginning to freak me out.

Then one of the ladies who appeared to be in charge explained to me that I was in fact, communicating with the devil. He, the devil, was showing himself as my Nana to trick me. It was the devil himself, they said.

I was devastated that they were saying these things to me, as my Nana and her visits were now very special to me. I had overcome my initial fears of seeing Spirit and had become used to her frequent visits. They made me feel very comfortable and loved.

Then there was a low hum in the room. These people all had their heads bowed and hands together and I realised they were all praying. I gathered from the words being spoken that they were praying for my soul.

This was a very daunting situation to be in. According to them, I was possessed by the devil. I could not leave, I had no idea where I was, I was in a locked room with all these strangers, and these people were now all praying for my soul.

I was terrified and felt nailed to the spot; I could not move.

This seemed to go on forever, and I must have been there for a few hours at least. It was the most confronting situation I had ever been in.

Eventually the praying stopped and the lady in charge announced the meeting was over.

The four of us left the house, got in the car and on the way home there were no words exchanged. I felt angry with my friend for putting me in this situation without fully explaining what the meeting was about or the type of group it was. It was a born-again Christian gathering.

Our friendship ended at that point, and we never saw each other again.

~❖~

Over time I have found out how reassuring it is to be able to talk to dead people and how uplifting, motivating, healing, and helpful it has been, for myself and many others. I had witnessed and experienced much of this at my own spiritualist church personally.

It was never my intention to become a medium or a teacher, but I do believe Spirit knew all the time that it would only be a matter of time before I was doing just that.

I had no idea that I would end up working this closely with the Spirit world. Helping others in so many ways; bringing their loved ones through with evidence only known to them and more importantly experiencing the healing that comes with that.

To be able to share my skills and teach others has become a passion of mine. I feel this is very important in order that we have a continual flow of new, well-trained mediums going out into the world. I would emphasise *good* mediums and *good* training. We want to continue the work of Spirit in the best possible way for all. That includes Spirit, the recipient, and the medium.

I think it is important is to bring reassurance to people that communicating with and seeing Spirit should not be scary but rather the most wonderful and natural thing in the world.

When you have lost a very close person to you in your life, their physical body has gone, but that is NOT the end of them. Their energy, personality, love – the essence of them – cannot be destroyed.

To know that we can all make these connections if we try and, of course, if we have the right guidance and teachers.

Einstein says that energy cannot be destroyed. Therefore, when our loved ones die and have lost their physical bodies, we can still contact them. This is done through their spiritual, energy body, which is the constant. This means your loved ones can continue to bring their love and guidance, in exactly the same way as they did when they were in the physical world.

They loved you when they were here, and that love remains with you. They do not want to see you suffering or struggling in any way and, therefore, they continue to bring the help and comfort that you need.

Mostly, people who were known to us in our physical lifetime have loved and taken care of us. When they pass to the spiritual world, the love and care remain without fail.

Most of us, when we arrive in the Spirit world, are excited that we are still 'alive', albeit as a Spirit person. We are excited when we become aware that we can continue to be around the loved ones we left behind.

When I have a Spirit communicating with me, they often acknowledge the joy and excitement they felt when that first connection happened to them.

Some people in our lives however, have not been good, supportive, or loving. When these people arrive in the Spirit world, they are made to realise, by Spirit guides and helpers, what mistakes they have made and they are then given the opportunity to grow into wisdom and with a new understanding of how to approach life's choices.

In my experience, when this is the case, these Spirits must help those still on earth by trying to redress the balance, to put things right, to let you know they are sorry.

These situations often create interesting connections until I explain this to the recipient. I have had a few people who say, "I don't want to connect to them."

This is one such story.

I had not long been doing spiritualist church services, but I was getting invitations from more and more of them.

As a medium, you are invited to a church, and as part of that service you have to bring accurate information through from the Spirit person, proving that they are the loved one of the person we are connecting to in the audience. For example: I have a man here, he tells me he is your dad. He had a heart attack, worked as an accountant, and smoked a pipe.

The evidence given by Spirit should be given accurately by the medium and the medium's words should reflect what the Spirit has said, not what the medium thinks they have said. This information has to be validated by the recipient as pertaining to that loved one. This is very important. The recipient needs proof that this IS their loved one communicating.

The medium is also expected to do the opening and closing prayers as well as the address or spiritual talk; this is like a sermon in a regular mainstream church like the Church of England.

I turned up at church for the service, as usual full of nerves and wanting to do my best for Spirit and the audience. It is a daunting thing, even now, to stand up in front of people who are expecting all the answers from you. All wanting a connection to their loved ones but knowing that you can only do so many in the allotted time.

The service was going well, and I had completed a few messages successfully. Then I brought a gentleman through who wanted to connect to his daughter. I was able to identify the young lady who the message was for and said to her, "I would like to come to you." I continued to give a description of this man and said, "He is your dad."

I was not prepared for what came next. She just screamed at me, "I don't want to talk to HIM!"

This was a totally new experience for me.

Panic set in. *What am I supposed to do here?* It was a daunting moment for me, and I have never forgotten it. It was one of those moments when you want the earth to swallow you up. But I stood firm and connected back to Spirit and asked the question. *What am I supposed to do here? Can you help me please? Is there someone else I can connect to?*

Then, almost immediately, I knew that Spirit was listening. This had all happened in an instant and I had to think on my feet.

Spirit took over; they were helping me, after all. I could feel it and it was wonderful. In stepped her nan. She was gorgeous, full of love. I could feel her and see her.

She gave me a description of herself. "I almost brought you up single-handed,"

"Yes," validated the young lady.

She continued, "I knitted really gawdy fair isle jumpers, which you hated, and I lived in a two-storey house, had a coal fire, which I taught you to lay for me. You hated getting the coal in when it was wet or dark as you were frightened of the dark. My birthday was 15 March, and my last birthday you bought me freesias that smelled too strong."

The young lady was in tears at this point. She was nodding yes to all that her nan was giving to me. She ended up with a really positive message.

I continued, "She tells me you have been really sad lately; you had an accident in your car, and she is telling me that because your insurance had run out, you were not able to get a new one to replace it."

I continued, "She says please don't worry, you have applied for a few new jobs, and the one you will get comes with a new car."

She finished with, "You were loved by so many people when you were growing up, but you were angry and didn't always believe their love was real. I need to tell you it was, and you didn't understand the full circumstances."

I got through the rest of the service and said my goodbyes to people as they were leaving. The young lady who had shouted at me came up to me in tears and asked, "Was that really my dad who came through? I feel terribly sorry that I didn't want to talk to him."

I told her that it was okay. "You were given the message you needed via your nan; it was the message your dad wanted me to give you."

She left in tears, but I knew these were tears of joy, knowing that her dad was still with her.

I felt the words 'didn't understand the full circumstances' were related to her dad and her own anger. I saw the healing that her message had given her instantly; it was visible to me and to others who were around her as she left the church.

Many people ask similar questions. What happens to us when we die? Are they alone? Are they with family? Were they there to meet them when they passed over? Are they taking care of them on the other side? Are they out of pain? Will they still be around me? Can I still talk to them?

Often there is much-unfinished business, things left unsaid. Some have guilt, thinking they had not done the right things for them before they died: I didn't get to say I'm sorry, or I love you, or I was not with them when they passed.

The pain that comes with this is huge, especially if they do not believe in the afterlife. But even those of us who do believe will ask similar questions. We just need to know they are okay now.

It's hard enough when we lose an adult, but when it comes to the death of a child, parents need to know that their baby is not floating around in the ether, and when alone they will ask you questions like: Is there someone looking after them? Will they grow up in the Spirit world? Will I see them when I pass? Will they still be around us?

Giving these parents that peace of mind is wonderfully healing.

Over my 30 years of doing this work, I have given many readings to people who have lost a child. They come through with such accurate information, confirming what they have seen in the house, how they have been commemorated, things they hear, plans being made, a bedroom that has been left untouched or confirming that their mum sits on their bed daily and talks to them.

These are some examples of a readings where a child has passed.

Another day of readings was booked at my home. I was awaiting the arrival of my next client. The lady arrived with her sister. She was in tears, looked remarkably small and crushed, and I thought on first sight that she must be at least ten years older than me. That's how her pain and grief had made her look and feel, inside and out.

I invited them into my lounge, where we all sat down. I made my connection to Spirit and her beautiful son came through. He was gorgeous and unusually lively. He shared information about his passing: "I was in an accident, a car and another larger vehicle, and I wasn't alone in the car; my friends were with me."

The lady confirmed it was her son. He then visually walked me around his bedroom at home, showing me all the things he loved. Then he said, "I can still play ball with my little brother."

She was laughing as she explained that he had been throwing a ball from the Spirit world and his little brother was catching it, then he was throwing it back to his brother in Spirit. Amazing! I had not come across a story like that before.

We sat and chatted with her son for nearly an hour. All the things I brought through from him were confirmed with such joy from his mum. I physically could see her Spirit lifting by the minute. The tears were now tears of joy, not the sadness that she had come in with.

She confirmed that he had been in an accident about ten weeks before this meeting and, as he had told me, "Mum was not at home when this had happened."

"Yes," she said.

The reading ended and it felt like my room was full of joy and love. The lady was not crumpled any more. She walked out of my house with the biggest smile on her face, standing straight, shoulders up and back, almost with a swagger of confidence. I could visibly see the years drop from her face. I found out later that she was ten years my junior.

This wonderful connection with her son, the information he brought through, proved to her that he was still there with her. To watch her physical transformation was heart-warming.

She and I have become good friends since this initial reading. She told me that was the first reading she had had after he passed. She is still most definitely sad at his loss and knows that nothing can bring him back, but knowing he is still around her, still sharing with the family, has brought her such joy and happiness. She knows he is okay and being looked after by family, and he continues to watch over them all.

In the early days of my mediumship, I was invited by a friend to go to a bereavement group for parents who had lost a child. My friend was a member of this group, as he had lost a child of his own.

I agreed to go along as it sounded interesting. I wanted to see for myself how people coped with such a loss. I wanted to experience loss from all angles.

When we arrived, we walked into a hall that was full of people, men and women and varying ages. They were all parents with that common thread of all losing a child.

The meeting started and people were sharing their experiences. The important point that I could see was the still painful common denominator, that they had lost 'their own' child. There was a large number of them there. I could feel their pain and grief. As they slowly shared their stories, one after the other, I felt very humbled. I sat there quietly observing and listening to the many stories.

We were all sitting in a circle, and I listened to each person who in turn gave their own experiences of loss, how they felt, how they were coping and the pain they were still feeling.

It didn't matter if it was a mum of 80 or a dad of 20, the loss was just as painful.

I was not prepared for the next story that was shared. A lady who said she had been to a medium. *That would be lovely*, I thought..... BUT

They had been charged £300. The lady was not satisfied with the information given to her and wanted more. The medium had told her, "If you pay me a further £300, I will be able to bring more information."

It may not sound like a lot of money now, but this was in the early 1990's, when £300 (AU$600) was a lot of money. Even by today's standards, this is a vast amount of money to pay for a reading. This 'if you pay me more' situation was disgusting. I was appalled. How was this allowed to happen? How could people be so unscrupulous when someone is this vulnerable?

I was shocked by what I was hearing. I was deeply embarrassed as a medium to be in that room. I was also very angry. This was not what mediumship was about.

My thoughts were that as a medium, we were supposed to be there to help people. These horrible so-called mediums were just preying on vulnerable people in their time of grief and loss. It was also giving them empty promises. I felt sick to my stomach. I did not dare say I was a medium; I was too ashamed of what these others had done. I just sat there quietly, listening as one after another of these people shared their similar stories. Sadly, people who take advantage are still out there.

This was one of the events that shaped my own mediumship. I wanted to make sure that I was truthful and honest and would never lead anyone on, lie, or make things up.

I never went back to the group because I was concerned they would always judge me through the lens of those dishonest mediums who came before me. For me this was a lesson I had to learn, knowing that not everyone is ethical or responsible with this work.

The readings done for people who have experienced the loss of a child can show how someones loss can help many people in many ways, once shared.

It was December when this couple booked for a reading, just before Christmas.

It was freezing in the UK, and although my home was toasty warm, when they sat down, they didn't remove their coats, which was interesting, and I thought it a bit strange.

I started talking to them about a previous reading that day, where the lady had said no to the information I was giving about a child coming through and how sad that was. I didn't realise why I was telling them this.

I told them, "And at the end of the reading, she had said, 'It's a shame my daughter didn't come through."

The couple were quiet, and I felt a bit sceptical. It was as if they were not sure what to expect. I tried to put their minds at ease as I chatted generally to them.

I like to make people feel comfortable when they come for a reading, as it can be a very emotional experience, as in this case. Sometimes they are not sure what to expect.

I then began to make my connections to Spirit and straight away realised why I had told them of the earlier lady who was very sceptical and regrettably denied her daughter.

Then there, by my side, looking up at me with the most beautiful big blue eyes, was a curly haired, blond, cherub-like little boy who looked to be around 2 years old.

I described this little boy, and they looked at each other. I said, "I believe this little boy is your son."

He was indeed their son, who had passed only a few weeks previously.

The reading was beautiful and full of emotion. "Your mum is standing here and telling me that she is looking after him for you both. She tells me she was waiting for him."

"Yes, my mum has passed," said the lady, tears starting to stream down her cheeks.

"Your son is showing me a wooden fire engine, and I am being told it's in his bedroom and it keeps moving on its own."

"Yes," said Dad.

"Mum and your son are laughing; we are playing with it and pushing it across the room."

Then the lady's mum said, "There is a new baby."

"Yes," they said in unison. The lady then unbuttoned her coat to show me she was indeed pregnant.

"Mum tells me you will see a red rose in the next week."

"But this is December, no roses bloom at this time of the year," he replied.

"Well, I can't change what she is telling me; please take it and see what happens, as I know she is right."

At the end of a very emotional reading for all of us, they left. They appeared much happier than when they had first arrived.

I say 'for all of us', as that included me. This was one of the most touching readings I had ever done, and I cried on and off for over a week.

A few weeks later, I got an email from them to say they had gone to visit his sister. They had been walking in the garden and there at the bottom of her garden was a bare rose bush with one red rose on it.

For these parents, all this information, plus much more, proved to them their little boy was still with them. The dad went on to write a book for parents who had lost a child, about how to cope with grief and loss.

CHAPTER 7

Our Transition to Spirit

People ask me what happens to us when we pass over to Spirit. I believe that when we arrive in Spirit, firstly, our physical body has gone, as we don't need it anymore. Then I have heard that our energy splits. This is like shining a light through a prism, which changes the light and shows us rainbows from each surface of the prism.

The white light is separated into its component colours: red, orange, yellow, green, blue, and violet. The separation of visible light into its different colours is known as dispersion or refraction.

If we imagine that on arrival in the Spirit world, we are the light being shone through a prism, our Spirit separates in a similar way. This has been explained to me by Spirit that we can be in different places, doing different things at the same time in the Spirit world. This is now our collective Spirit.

After physical death, each part of that collective Spirit can choose what comes next. This could be:

- healing those left behind from the loss

- still giving their guidance in our physical world

- letting family know they are okay

- letting the deceased Spirits know they are not alone but surrounded by other family members in Spirit

- healing from whatever took us over. This period of time varies, depending on the Spirit, the type of death, and many other factors. Some Spirits do not come through straight away, some never return, and others come the same day.

We move on in the spiritual realms, continually learning and progressing, 'moving up the spiritual ladder', if you like. Progression of our soul is important. These lessons, according to Native Americans, will continue until we reach the point of being a 'pure soul', at which point we move into the higher realms.

People like Brian Weiss have written many books on reincarnation and past life regression. Using hypnosis, they can take a person back to a point before this life. In Brian Weiss's books, there is a lovely tale of two people, male and female, who have never met in this life; they live on opposite sides of the USA. They are both clients of his, and under hypnosis he is listening to the same stories. She was his father in a previous life and he was the daughter. Fascinating and worth reading.

If it's time for our Spirit to rest at this time, then we can choose to do this. And if that resting means sitting on a riverbank and fishing all day, then that's okay, too.

The spiritual realm can look like whatever you want it to be. For example, if you loved to knit and sit in front of a roaring fire when you were here, you can do exactly this!

I have heard many reports from Spirit about what happens through my own personal readings, the readings I do for others, and the many books I have read over the years.

When we are born, people here on earth are excited to be greeting a new baby and have big celebrations.

At the same time in the Spirit world, they are sad, if you like, to see Spirits leave the Spirit world.

The same goes for us losing someone here on earth; when someone has died, we are very sad to see them go, for their loss.

However, in the Spirit world they are delighted to welcome them back home.

As Spirit are around us constantly, they are aware of what is happening in our physical world, for instance, when someone is sick or when it is time for them to return home to Spirit, and there will be that welcoming party. We always are met by our loved ones when we return to Spirit.

There are lots of stories I have heard, where even though the loved one was in excruciating pain before they died, as they pass over their faces suddenly appear peaceful, all that pain gone, and a smile appears on their face. They have seen their loved ones who are waiting for them, and they are being beckoned into the Spirit world by Spirits they recognise. It is then okay for the dying person to let go and transition to the Spirit world.

Not long after being in Spirit, we are aware of being able to remain around loved ones in the physical world. Of course, it's a different energy level, but still they can continue to help us. This is a beautiful thing for both sides, knowing that we continue to be able to help, guide, and comfort.

This can be shown from some of the examples I have included this book. The love and help that these connections bring is extremely reassuring.

CHAPTER 8

Bad and Evil Spirits

I don't want to put too much energy into this subject of bad and evil Spirits, but I feel that it needs to be mentioned as I get asked questions about this regularly.

I am sure most of you have heard of good and bad Spirits. In the entire 30-plus years that I have been working with Spirit, I have only ever had good Spirits around me.

I believe it is up to us individuals to put the intention around us that you want to work with love, light, and good, and then only good Spirits will work with you. It's that simple.

I have been told many times by others, "You have a negative entity attached to your aura."

To which I answer, "No, I don't."

These people have been quite insistent at times, but I would ask, "Can you prove that there is an attachment there?"

It's only what they are seeing. You cannot actually see it; I believe it's in the mind of the person who says they are seeing it.

When you are connecting to Spirit, you can prove with the evidence you, as the medium, is giving to the recipient. If the information is correct, you get a yes, and if not, you get a no. You are getting that validation from the recipient.

With an attachment, how can this be proved? I have never seen one. Therefore, for me they are not there, not in my sacred space. I do not allow anything other than good Spirits or energies into my sacred space.

This also follows when giving a reading. I can see if your energy is dull, maybe there is stress or illness for instance, but I will not turn that into something negative for the recipient.

I could say, "Oh, I feel there is a blockage in your energy," or "I feel a sadness with you," or "You do not appear to be feeling yourself." Never would I turn that into, "You have an attachment," or "You are going to die soon," or "Life is not worth living."

I see too much of this. That is a medium or psychic who is working from their own energy or head space and not working with Spirit energy. Why would Spirit, who are there to help us, tell us anything bad? That's not the way it works, as far as I'm concerned.

There is a positive way of giving this, too: "You are feeling a little blocked, but that means there's a need for change around you," or "Let go of the sadness, surround yourself with happy, positive people, and be happy in yourself," or "You have allowed people to affect your energies and your life; step out of their way and make your life the best way you can."

My thought is Spirit are around us, surrounding us with love, positivity, and encouragement. If we are working with pure intent, why would bad, negative Spirits be allowed in? It just does not make any sense to me.

I think people like scare-mongering in a lot of cases. These are people who like to think they can be better than you, know more than you, but it is just filling people's minds with fear.

There is much information on the internet about bad and evil Spirits, but none of it has been properly researched or validated. To me it shows an ignorance in your spiritual education and just someone trying to prove they know more than you do, which is ego.

If you are ever told such things, please don't believe them.

Whether I am working with Spirit or not, I create a sacred space for myself. The reason I do this is we do not know what energies we are going to come up against as we go through our day.

I am not saying that there are evil people around us, but there are those who do have issues that we can't always see. As sensitives, we can pick up on that energy. For instance, you may have crossed paths with someone who has just learned of a death. Their energy is full of sadness and despair; this is what we could pick up on.

My sacred space is like a bubble of protection. By having that bubble around us, we don't allow the energy of others to rub off on us or enter our auric energy field.

I have read many books by medium and healer Betty Shine. In my early days, her books were my bibles, especially the *Mind* series. They were simple and very easy to understand. I loved them and still do. They are worth reading, as I know they can help in your mediumship and spiritual development.

You simply visualise a giant balloon in front of you, step into it, and then zip it up. Then you know you have protection around you.

You can fill it with a colour of your choice if you want, and whatever colour you choose, this will be the healing or protection that you need at that exact time.

CHAPTER 9

Chakras and Auras

The colours of our chakras and auras have a great significance. This is a brief explanation of how I perceive them.

The chakra body is our spiritual body. If our physical and spiritual bodies are not in alignment, we have dis-ease.

Relating to your mediumship, if you are having issues with your connections to Spirit, it could be that your chakras are not aligned properly. Therefore, taking the time to balance these chakras is important in order to make those connections better and easier.

Relating to your health, again blockages can cause various illnesses.

Chakra balancing should be done regularly.

I know that when my physical energies were depleted, so too were my spiritual energies. It took a long time and a lot of work to get that balance right, but I persisted, and it worked, and Spirit helped with this, too.

Chakra Colours

I list here the chakra names, their associated colours, and their focus.

Root – red – grounding, stability

Sacral – orange – sensuality, creativity, strength, motivation

110 | *5 minutes more*

Solar plexus – yellow – emotions

Heart – pink/green – love

Throat – blue – communication

Third Eye – purple – clear seeing

Crown – silver/white – connection to Spirit

The Aura

We all have an auric energy field surrounding our physical body, which is like an electrical field. When you can see this with the physical eye, you will see many colours.

This does take practice though; like the 'magic pictures' in the 1970s, you have to train your eyes to see them. These colours indicate how we are in ourselves, our health, mental state, or spiritually.

An envelope of vital energy, which radiates from everything in nature: minerals, plants, animals, and humans. The aura is not visible to normal vision but may be seen by clairvoyance as a halo of light. Then it often appears as a multi-coloured mist that fades off into having sparks, rays, and streamers.
—Martin Parsons

Do you get a sense of people's energy? How does that feel to you? Is it a scratchy feeling, or does it feel nice? Or, when you meet a certain type of person, do they drain you, depleting your own energies? This is you sensing people's auras.

Guided meditation helps you to use your imagination; visualisation gives you the ability to see things that are supposedly not there. The more you practice this, the better.

Some of us have logical thinking brains, and it may be for you more difficult to trust these images, but please do give it a try.

Aura Colours

I list here the aura colours and their focus.

Red – well-grounded, energetic, strong-willed

Orange – adventurous, thoughtful, considerate

Yellow – creative, relaxed, friendly

Green – social, communicator, nurturing

Blue – intuitive, spiritual, freethinker

Indigo – curious, spiritually connected, gentle

CHAPTER 10

Colours and Significance

On the occasions when I saw my Nana after her passing, she was always dressed in orange. My brother and sisters saw her dressed in orange, too. Strange that we all saw her in the same colour. What could that colour indicate?

I didn't realise how important colours are in the Spirit world till much later in my spiritual journey. I believe orange is a very spiritual colour, signifying strength, motivation, and determination.

I have also seen orange described this way:

- Orange is the colour of the sacral chakra, which relates to creativity, sensuality, and our emotional subtle body. Orange is the energy centre for exchange and relationships, placing high value on friendships and interacting with others. People will:

- resonate with the vibrations of joyful exchange, whether relating to work, resources, money, time, energy, or love

- possess strength in teamwork due to their ability to be relatable and sociable

- be highly perceptive and incredibly dynamic individuals

- these friendships develop very quickly for relationship experts.

These are some examples of seeing Spirit and what those sightings mean.

My youngest sister came to visit us in Cornwall with her best friend when she was about 14. I was living in a very small, two-bedroom house. Therefore, the girls had to sleep downstairs on a mattress in the living room.

One morning when I got up, my sister asked, "Why did you come down in the night?"

"I didn't," I said.

She said, "Yes, you did – you opened the door, stepped into the room, and stood there looking at us. You didn't say anything. Then you went out, closed the door, and I heard you walking up the stairs."

"I didn't come down at all," I said.

Then I had a thought – if it wasn't me, who or what could it have been?

"Can you describe what I was wearing?"

"You had an orange dressing gown on," she told me.

"But I don't own an orange dressing gown," I said.

She went on to give more of a description of the things she could remember.

"Oh, my goodness," I said. "That was Nana. You have never met her, but I have been seeing her for years."

There were ten years between my sister and me, and I was 7 when I first started seeing Nana. This was the first time my sister had seen Nana in Spirit.

The colour was relating to my sister, and I feel it was to do with some emotional issues she was going through at that time.

This was more confirmation for me that my Nana was still there, keeping a watchful eye over my little sister. Her visit was to let my sister know this.

My brother came to visit on another occasion. He knew Nana but would have only been around 4 years old when she passed to Spirit.

One morning he got up early as he was going fishing. We were sitting in the kitchen having tea and toast. He seemed to want to say something but looked awkward.

"Are you okay?" I said.

"Something odd happened last night," he said finally. "I was woken up by something moving on my bed." He hesitated, and then continued, "When I focused my eyes to the dark, I realised it was Nana sitting there, smiling at me."

My brother was a man of few words and very much the sceptical type, and I could see he was struggling with what he was telling me.

"Before I knew it," he continued, "we were having full-blown conversation, it was like she was really there, but I know she's dead."

I laughed as he said this. He added, "She told me that I was getting engaged soon... How could she know that? I only just decided and haven't told anyone yet."

I asked him to describe her.

"She had an orange dress of some sort and red hair with a white stripe on the top of her head," he told me.

I went upstairs and dug out a photo of Nana and showed it to him. "Yes, that's her," he said.

He was a little less sceptical after this and in fact shared with me other visits that Nana had made to him.

My first marriage had ended, and a while after I married again and moved to London. We had been trying for a baby for a short time, and one morning I woke up and just knew that I was pregnant. *My intuition is working here*, I thought.

But then I saw Nana standing by my side, and I wasn't completely sure if she was real or in my head. I just knew she was there talking to me. "You are having a baby," she said, "and it's going to be a girl this time." I already had two boys.

I was extremely excited but thought I should keep it quiet until I had done a test. One thing I was sure about, and I'm sure it was her influence – I had to choose Victoria for her name. I didn't know at the time where that came from.

What I didn't know at that time was Nana, who we all knew to be called Hilda, was really called Victoria Hilda. This really surprised me; I never knew.

After I had Victoria, I let people know she was here. A little while later my Aunty Lynn, Nana's eldest daughter, rang me.

She told me, "Nana would have been so very proud that you have chosen the name Victoria." She continued, "I promised my mum that I would call my first daughter Victoria, but for some reason I changed my mind at the last minute. Mum was very disappointed."

She carried on very excitedly, "Mum got her wish, only a little later on down the family line."

We both had a giggle about it, and I related the story of how the name came about.

My dad's mum and dad died, respectively, when I was 7 and 16. Mum's parents died when I was in my 30's. I have had many visits from all of my grandparents over the years, and they always seem to come when there is a need. This could be from excitement, health, or emotional issues. Their visits have always been extremely comforting to me. I thank them constantly.

I moved into a house that needed renovations. It had been lived in for over 45 years by an old man called Eric. The house was still decorated in colours from the 1960/70's. Lots of brown and orange. These had to go, and as I was on my own and short on money, I would have to do much of it myself.

When I was growing up, I always loved to help my dad with jobs around the house, and on his car, too. He taught me well, and I was not afraid to tackle most jobs on my own. I often told him, "I should have been a boy," which always made him laugh.

This day in my new home, with a lot of the repairs done, it was time to lay a new laminate/floating floor. I had completed the main rooms downstairs and upstairs; I was left with the hallway and around the bottom of the stairs.

I had never attempted anything like this before. The straight lines in the other rooms had been easy enough, but the hallway was a different story – so many corners and curves. I was not going to give up. I made heaps of mistakes throwing aside many odd bits of flooring.

I was now getting frustrated. *Who could help me with this?* That's when Grandad, on Mum's side, popped into my head. *Why didn't I think to ask him before now?*

I stood there and asked, "I am stumped with this, and I really could do with your help, please."

Then I got on with finishing the job, with the last bit being the very awkward shape at the bottom of the staircase. This was very difficult indeed.

I am a very stubborn person and would not give up. But when I had finished, it looked brilliant – if you didn't look too closely, that is!

Aching from head to foot, I headed to bed. I could not straighten my poor body and every part of me ached.

Then, suddenly, as I got to the top of the stairs, I was shocked to hear my Grandad's voice very clearly. I heard him say to me, "Well done, Val, great job!"

It was his voice, loud and clear, not my imagination. He had a very distinctive voice, and I could not have mistaken it.

My Grandad had been a carpenter for many years, and knowing that he had been watching me, had listened to my pleas for help and no doubt tried to help, filled me with overwhelming joy. I slumped to the floor as tears slipped down my cheek.

He had listened, he had helped, and he was congratulating me on a job well done. I fell into bed and had a blissful night's sleep.

I felt very proud of myself and thankful that he had been there with me, guiding me. Thank you again, Grandad.

My lovely grandparents have all been with me ever since, coming through in many messages via other mediums and students, as well as communicating directly with me.

I had heard that one of my aunties recently died. We were not that close, and I hadn't seen her for a few years. This happens with families, sadly.

I was on a day off from work and was at home on my own. I had just got in the shower and clearly heard a lady's voice, as clear as a bell. It was as if she was in the same room as me. The voice was telling me to phone Hazel."

I knew then that this voice would be Aunty Dorothy. She wanted me to get through to her daughter Hazel.

I heard the message but thought, *This is an odd time to call Hazel; she'll be at work.*

They had their own business and worked very long hours. She would be at work now...but my aunt had sounded very insistent that I call. I got out of the shower, wrapped a towel around my hair and another around my body, and went to the phone to call my cousin.

To my complete surprise, the phone rang a few times, and then Hazel picked up. I did the normal pleasantries, "Hi, Hazel, how are you doing?"

She replied, "I am not in a good place, Val. I'm not well and really missing Mum."

I could tell that she had been crying, as she was snuffly, and I could hear the sobs. "I was just sitting here with Mum's head scarf on my lap. She had it on when she passed, and I took it as a keepsake."

I explained to her why I was calling. "I heard your mum's voice clearly telling me to ring you. I was in the shower when this happened." Then I said, "I'm sitting here dripping all over the living room," at which she laughed.

We hadn't seen each other for some time, and she was not aware of the work I was doing with Spirit.

My cousin was rather happy and very grateful that I had passed this message on to her.

We chatted about her mum and how my cousin was feeling and shared some lovely family memories. "Mum wanted you to know that she is okay," I told her, "out of her pain, and still around all the family, watching over you."

As I finished, she said, "Oh Val, thank you for calling me and sharing Mum's message. It was just what I needed today."

Isn't it funny how things work out?

As I was just writing this story, my other cousin, Mo, popped into my head. Mo is Hazel's sister and sadly has cancer, for which she is going through treatment. Her mum just popped into my head, and I thought, *I better call Mo.*

She answered, which I was surprised about in the first place as she never answers her phone. She told me, "I'm at the hospital having my treatment."

I told her, "Well I had to ring you now, as your mum is here and prompted me to do so. She wants to let you know she is there with you."

Mo and her daughter, who was with her at the time, were extremely happy and grateful for that 'little' message.

Magical, I thought.

~❖~

It was coming up to my father-in-law's 60th birthday. What gift to get him – that was a tricky one.

His mum had died when he was 18 months old, and he had been brought up by his grandmother and two aunties.

We had come down from London to Wales that weekend to try and sort out a present for Dad for his special birthday.

We were wracking our brains, and then his son said, "What about the one photograph of his mum that's up in the attic?" We went up at the first opportunity to check it out.

The frame was damaged, the glass broken, and the photograph had been damaged, too. We quickly rang around to see if there was someone who could fix this up, and we were in luck. I found a shop that could repair not only the frame but also replace the glass and fix the damage to the photograph.

Very sneakily, and without Dad's knowledge, we managed to take the picture and frame from the house.

When we were in Wales, we usually tried to take the opportunity to visit the old aunties who had brought Dad up. They were both getting on in years. We told them what we were doing with Dad's present, and they were quite emotional on hearing it.

Then, without a word, one of them rose from her chair and disappeared. When she returned from her bedroom, she handed us a wedding ring.

She said, "This was the ring that belonged to Dad's mum." We realised the enormity of this gesture for them. They had kept it all those years, waiting for the appropriate time to give it to Dad.

Coincidence or not, this was the day we were to collect the newly framed picture, which we did on our way back to Dad's.

When we returned, we gathered the family, got out the champagne, and gave him his present.

Dad was always a very emotional man, but I don't think he could believe what he was seeing. He was lost for words, and tears filled his eyes.

Then we told him that him about the wedding ring. "When we visited your aunties today, they gave us this to give to you." We handed him his mum's ring. I think we were all in tears that day. It really was a momentous and emotional day.

After a long, happy day, we all went to bed. When we got up in the morning, when we were gathered around the breakfast table, I could not contain myself. "I have to tell you all what I experienced last night."

I continued, "I was fast asleep when I was suddenly woken up by a very tiny framed Spirit person sitting on my bed. It was a lady; I knew that as I smelled her perfume, which was quite sweet."

Everyone was just looking at me. There were mixed feelings about the work I was doing with Spirit. However, I carried on as I was extremely excited.

"She sat beside me on the edge of the bed and then stretched her arm out across my sleeping body, which she placed on the other side of me."

There were all looking at me with their mouths open. "I didn't feel uncomfortable or scared by this; she made me feel calm and peaceful. I feel it may have been your mum come to say she was acknowledging the birthday presents that had been given to you yesterday. I felt her happiness and emotions."

Well, that story was enough, I thought.

After I had finished telling of my experience, my son suddenly spoke up. "I had the exact same thing happen to me," he said, "and like your lady, Mum, this one was a tiny lady."

Dad's mum was the tiniest of ladies. Her portrait confirmed that.

Such confirmation from her that this was Dad's mum coming in to say thank you. She had come home to be with her son on his special day. The three things together – the picture, the ring, and the birthday – had all made this possible. She was happy, and so was he. The picture now stands in pride of place in his home.

CHAPTER 11

My Family's Experience With Spirit

When my boys were about 4 and 5, we moved to a house near the seaside, in a beautiful little village called Ogmore-by-Sea. It was our dream home. However, it wasn't long after we moved in that we started having some really weird things taking place.

It had started as a little stone cottage, but previous owners had added to it several times, which had made it into a very strange shape. The main room to the house was long and narrow with French windows at the far end, leading out onto the garden. All the bedrooms adjoined this main room, except ours. There was a tiny square hallway in between the lounge and our bedroom. The kitchen and bathroom were at the back of the house.

At night, as you do, we always locked up, front and back doors. But a number of times we would wake up in the morning to find the front door wide open. We checked with the boys, and they had not done this.

On one of these occasions, we awoke to find sheep in the little hallway (we lived on common grazing land where the sheep roamed free).

One beautiful sunny evening in July, we had my nephew staying with us, and all the boys who were similar ages wanted to watch the new Superman video.

We sat them down with bowls full of goodies to watch the film. They were all pretty excited.

As we were sitting watching the film, there was a knock on the French windows (which were in front of us), but we could see that there was no one at the door. We decided to ignore it. Then there came another knock, louder this time. Then to our absolute horror, the doors started rattling quite violently. But still we could see there was no one there.

My husband and I looked at one another. He got up to see what was going on, and I followed.

We didn't want to alarm the boys, who were totally engrossed in the movie.

As we walked through the room towards the French doors, both of us felt someone or something push past us. Both doors leading to our bedroom opened on their own. This spooked us both very much.

The next few weeks brought even more spooky happenings.

The boy's bedroom was on the opposite side of the lounge to ours. As we lived in a tiny village, there were not many outside lights, so it was dark at night. We used to keep the light on at night-time, just in case the boys woke up.

One night when we were all fast asleep, I suddenly woke up as I was aware of the blankets at the end of the bed being lifted. There were little hands, like those of a child, touching my toes. My mind and heart were both racing, but I did not dare open my eyes! *What on earth is this?*

If it had been the boys coming into our room, the light from the hallway would be shining in my eyes. But there was no light! I forced myself to go back to sleep. There had to be a logical explanation. Was I dreaming?

I must have dropped off to sleep, and then suddenly my husband leapt out of bed, screaming. "Something touched me!"

he shouted, describing exactly what I had felt, the blanket lifting and the tiny hands. He was terrified.

We got up and checked the whole house. The boys were still fast asleep in their beds. All the doors and windows were locked; nothing was out of the ordinary.

I often got the smell of flowery perfume in the house. I hate flowery perfume, therefore it couldn't have been mine!

A few days after this incident, I was in the house on my own and busy in the kitchen doing my housework. Then, out of the blue, a milk bottle smashed in the sink, all five doors off the main living room slammed shut, and the plant box in front of the French windows fell over, scattering plants and earth everywhere.

This all happened at exactly the same time. This really scared me; there were no explanations.

What is happening? Neither of us had any idea.

The tiny village we lived in was on the coast, very old and with a long history of ghostly tales. There were pirates and wreckers. These were people who lured the ships onto the rocks, and then when they had run aground, the ships were looted and any survivors killed.

I thought I would mention these happenings to the locals in the village pub and see if they could shed any light on what was happening to us and our house.

They regaled us with many stories about the ghosts in the area, and there were many.

Apparently our house had been built on the site of an old Quaker meeting place. One man who lived next door said, "There have been many sightings of a ghostly woman walking up our lane leading to your property and then through the house. I have seen her a few times and she is dressed in grey; she wears some sort of bonnet or hat and is really tiny."

Another man told us, "The previous owners of the house were a little odd. They delved in black magic and other spooky stuff."

Listening to these tales really alarmed us both. We decided that something had to be done, but what?

At this time in my life, I was not using my own psychic / spiritual abilities, and I certainly had no idea what was happening. I knew something was there but not the reason why. It was not like the sightings I had of my Nana, which filled me with love and joy. This felt totally different, and we were both unsettled by it.

I had heard of exorcisms, and I did a bit of research. There was no internet like we have today, meaning it was a trip to the library and poring over many books. My husband was a Catholic and I thought I would call the local Catholic Church, which I did the next day.

I was put through to the Canon of the church, who had a very calm, gentle voice. I explained to him what had been going on and why I was concerned. "I don't know where to turn," I said. "These things have been going on for a while now." I explained to him in detail what had been happening and how it was making us feel.

To my surprise, he was very understanding. "I can come out this afternoon if that's convenient," he said.

He told us he was going to carry out a blessing on the house. Sounded like something out of a movie, but we felt we needed to do this and were willing to try anything.

The Canon walked around our home, saying prayers in Latin and sprinkling holy water as he went. We quietly followed him, listening intently.

The next few days were interesting, it was as if the energy in the house had changed, and the happenings stopped. Whatever the Canon had done appeared to be working.

After years of working with Spirit, I look at things very differently now.

At the time we had been going through a very difficult time in our marriage, and it was like someone was trying to warn me about the situation I was in. I was not listening; I didn't want to listen, and didn't recognise the signs that were being shown to me.

If this was to happen to me now, I would have approached it in a different way. Now I would have carried out a house clearing. Moving on any unwanted Spirits, which I have done many times.

But at the time I did not understand what was taking place; it just scared us all.

Spirit was indeed trying to warn me, as events that came up shortly afterward would change my life forever.

When fear steps in, it's hard to think rationally. I would like to think that now there would be no fear, and I would certainly be questioning what was going on in a different way.

I wonder how many of us have things happening and not realised it could be a loved one from Spirit trying to say, "Hey, I'm here for you," or "I can help." We really should be more aware of their efforts to try to help us!

This story is confirmation of Spirit being around. They knew there was something wrong and tried to help us fix it. They tried to show us in many ways that there was something not right, but this story was like a jigsaw puzzle for us to put together. We got there in the end, which was a huge relief. The consequences here would have been disastrous if Spirit had not worked their magic and persisted. This was a series of events that led us to the problem and a solution.

I was at home alone, full of excitement as all my family was gathering for a pre-Christmas weekend. I was getting on with normal chores and washing glasses. I'm terrified of glass breaking and always take great care. As I concentrated on washing each as carefully as I could, suddenly one glass shattered in my hand. It broke into little squares, completely shattered.

I instantly threw the glass down and shouted at Spirit, "I don't like that! What's this all about?" I felt their presence and wanted to know why they were there and if there was a link to the breaking glass. Nothing came from them.

The following day, a Saturday, my daughter and I were preparing dinner. This year would be a strange Christmas as the whole family was going to be in different places for Christmas Day, so

I decided to do Christmas early – the tree, the decorations and presents, the lot.

I was going to be in Wales, my two sons, Gareth in America, Neil in England, and Victoria in Australia.

My daughter had already realised the day before that she had left her passport at university and would have to make a special two-hour trip to collect it. She and I were both travelling from Heathrow in three days time, her to Australia and me to Israel.

As we were preparing the vegetables, suddenly she said, "Oh, someone walked right through me." She thought it was one of her brothers teasing her, but the boys were both in the other room.

When I personally feel Spirit around me, I always acknowledge them.

I told her, "Say hello and thank you for being there," to Spirit. She reluctantly did.

We carried on preparing dinner and talking when suddenly the conversation changed in a heartbeat.

We were back to talking about her passport. Again it had come up. She was really annoyed with herself that she had forgotten to bring it home with her.

Then she said, "I'm really glad it doesn't run out until February."

The sudden realisation of that statement hit me. I knew from my own extensive travelling that you needed to have at least six months left on your passport to be able to travel. She was obviously not aware of this. Panic set in as we went about trying to sort this out.

She immediately got on the phone to the passport office, which confirmed that a minimum of six months was required. "But today is Saturday!" she said in a high-pitched voice to the man on the phone, "and all the passport offices are closed on the weekend."

The earliest appointment we could get in London was the following Tuesday. This was no good as she was supposed to be travelling early that day. Her feeling of panic was growing by the second.

After much discussion with the man in the passport office, we managed to get an appointment on Monday morning at 8 am in Wales.

I was trying to keep everyone calm but having great difficulties in doing so.

Talk about all being at the last minute. Her passport had to be collected from Brighton University on Sunday, and we had to drive from Brighton to Wales that night in order to get her new passport on the Monday morning. Opposite ends of the country. That was a very long, stressful day.

We finally got back from Wales late Monday night with the new passport and a wallet that was a lot lighter. Because this was an emergency passport, it cost a lot more than normal.

We were all able to fly out as arranged on Tuesday morning.

I realise that Spirit had been with us on the day of the glass breakage. When my daughter felt Spirit walking through her and then out of the blue bringing up the subject of the passport, twice. They were trying hard to get through to us that this was an issue.

I can't imagine how devastating it would have been if she had arrived at the airport to be told she could not travel. She would have had no one around to help here as we would have all left the country. But thanks to the Spirit world, this problem was solved.

It is wonderful to think that all the people I have known in this earthly life are around me watching and being at the ready when I need help. This goes for us all.

We all need to listen closer and to believe that Spirit can and do help.

Thanking them for their help and guidance when it comes is just as important.

I love when Spirit guides you to do things and you have no idea why, but when I get these feelings now, I tend to just go along with it, as I have found them always to be right.

You can call it intuition, a knowing, or just a funny feeling. This was one of those occasions. Spirit worked hard to get us to pay attention, and in the end we did.

My Nana and Grandad on my mum's side were Londoners, but due to health reasons they moved to Wales to live with my mum. They were with her for the last 15 years of their lives. It was wonderful to have them that close after living so far away from us all.

Coming up to Christmas 1987, I hadn't been planning on going to Wales for Christmas, but something was nagging at me. I felt I needed to go home for a visit. I decided to pay attention to that nagging feeling.

It was good to see everyone, but I knew this wasn't the reason for those feelings I was getting. Everyone appeared to be in good health, including Nan and Grandad.

I loved hearing Nan and Grandad's stories, of which there were many. Grandad certainly liked to talk. I loved spending time with them. However, my visit came to an end, and I returned home to London.

I still had no idea why the urgency to go down to see them – what was that? At this time, I was not used to Spirit warning me or preparing me.

However, two weeks later, Grandad died unexpectedly. We were all shocked. He was 87, and although he had previous health issues, at this time he was as fit as a fiddle and very active.

I returned home for his funeral and was amazed that a man who loved to tell stories had kept so many remarkable ones to himself.

At the service they talked of his bravery and courage during WWII. He and a fellow soldier had escaped from a prisoner of war camp, and as they headed to Allied territory had mapped out all the munitions dumps along the way. When they eventually got to their destination, they handed the map to the Allies, who bombed all these dumps.

He didn't talk about his war days, as they were too painful. Yet, listening to this story I knew his actions had saved thousands of lives. I felt very proud of him.

It looked like I had been sent there to say my goodbyes without realising that was what that feeling had been. I would have been kicking myself had I not gone.

Sometimes, and we all do this, we make the silliest of excuses not to do things and then question why we didn't follow our gut instinct.

In the weeks that followed, Nan was naturally devastated by his death. They had been together for over 60 years and had never been separated apart from Grandad's time in WWII. Her health started to deteriorate at this time, and sadly for my mum, Nan had to be put into a nursing home to be cared for.

There it was again, this nagging feeling inside that I should go down to Wales to visit her. I was paying attention this time.

It was a lovely visit. I walked in and she looked incredibly frail. "Hello Nan," I said, "how are you doing?"

She was so happy to hear my voice. Nan had been blind for over 15 years. "What are you doing here?" she said. "It's a long way for you to come."

"I wanted to see how you were doing, and I have a surprise for you," I told her.

She loved her London treats; one of these was jellied eels. "I have brought you two tubs of jellied eels." She squealed with delight.

I got a tray for her and watched the happiness on her face as she devoured the two tubs. "Oh, Val, they were delicious and really fresh," she said. "Where did you get them from?"

"I had to do some searching, that's for sure." We both laughed. She was really happy as we sat there chatting.

I had been telling her about the work I had been doing recently, churches and readings. She had never shown an interest before, but out of the blue she asked, "How many churches are there?" My answer only piqued her interest more.

Then she asked, "What is you do and how do you do it?"

On and on the questions went: How many people believed? How many went to these churches? How many churches were there?

We sat there for a long time as I shared this information with her the best I could. I told her about my training, the qualifications I had, and that I was a spiritual minister.

"I never realised that you had done all that, Val, how wonderful," she said. "You are so clever." Then she asked, "Does that mean I will see Grandad again and we will be together?" The thought brought tears to both our eyes.

She wanted that confirmation. I feel she knew her own time was coming to an end, and with this came a fear. She wanted to know that there was more to life than just this life!

I then said to her, "Grandad is around you always, Nan. He is here now, telling you not to be frightened as he will be waiting for you."

Her face just lit up. It was like a weight had been lifted from her shoulders, and her gorgeous smile said it all to me. She was happy and content with what I had told her.

We carried on chatting for a while, and then I told her I had to leave. She said, "Thank you, Val. You are very special to me, and your comforting words today have helped me so much. Thank you again."

Many tears were flowing now, but I knew they were tears of joy.

She just needed to be convinced she would see the love of her life again. That day I left a much happier Nan. I didn't know that it would be the last time I would see her.

Two weeks later my Nan died, just six weeks after her husband. I personally think she died of a broken heart as she couldn't bear to be without him.

But I was delighted that I had the opportunity before she died to share a little understanding of the Spirit world with her. Spirit yet again had directed me, and I listened. I feel lucky that I did that.

They have both come through from Spirit many times, which brings me such joy and happiness.

CHAPTER 12

Mary's Help for Book and More

It was a beautiful summer's day in July in the UK, and I was enjoying soaking up some sun, watching my colourful Koi Karp playfully jumping for food in the pond in my back garden.

I was suddenly aware that someone was standing next to me. I looked up and there was my beautiful friend Mary. I said, "Hello, Mary," then, "Oh, Maaaaaary…"

She was a wonderful friend and supporter of me and my work, and I had been devastated that for the past few months she had been very sick.

I was suddenly hit by the realisation that *if you are standing here, you must have died.*

She looked very happy, as she usually did. She also looked very normal, as if she was really standing there watching the fish with me. I was sad to know that she had died but I was very relieved that she was now out of her pain.

Mary had run Ewell Spiritualist Chapel in Surrey, which was a wonderful spiritualist gathering. She had made it this way with her beautiful, no-nonsense attitude, and it ran like clockwork each week. She was the best. I loved her dearly, as did many others.

She was a very brash and outspoken Welsh lady with a heart of gold. She always said it as it was.

It used to make me smile at every service, as she would sing her heart out, but she couldn't sing. I often thought when I was standing there, *but all Welsh people can sing!*

She did such an incredible amount of work for Spirit, not just within the church.

After Mary's appearance in my garden, I went in to make a cup of tea, and within the hour her daughter called me. She said, "Mum has just passed."

I said, "I know, she has already been here." Her daughter was full of mixed emotions as I said this.

She said, "Of all people, I knew Mum would come to you." She was really happy about that.

Then, when she gathered her thoughts she asked me, "What are you going to do about Mum's funeral?"

I was a little surprised and responded, "What do you mean? Mum asked me to read at her funeral. Is that what you mean?"

She replied, "No, no. Mum told me before she passed that you were doing the funeral service for her."

Wow, that was a shock and complete news to me.

I had never been asked to carry out a funeral before. Now it was my turn for mixed emotions. I was proud to be asked to honour my beautiful friend but terrified at the same time. *What will I have to do?*

I would have to do some research. All I could do was get on with it and ask for Spirit help – in fact, as much as they could provide.

Luckily enough – or was it Spirit intervention? I would like to think it was a bit of both – I had called in on Mary a few weeks earlier.

I had not seen her for a while, due to her illness, and wanted to see how she was doing. I rang her and a shaky-voiced Mary answered the phone. I was staggered to hear her sounding so frail and weak.

I asked her if I could pay her a visit, to which she said yes instantly. I then told her, "I have decided to write a book and would love you to share some of your own Spirit experiences with me that I can include." I knew from spending time with her that she had a lifetime of spooky events.

When I arrived, the door was opened by her daughter, who invited me into the living room, where I first set my eyes on Mary. I had not seen her since her illness started.

Oh, my goodness, it was such a shock. She was not just frail, but skin and bone. She wasn't a big lady before her illness, but this was awful to see. I tried hard not to show my feelings.

She greeted me in her normal jolly way, but I could see how much she was struggling to breathe.

"Do you mind if I record our chat?" I asked her. "I'll forget things if I don't; you know me, I have a head like a sieve." I continued, "I know how important these stories are going to be to my book." She giggled, knowing me very well.

Her daughter brought us a cup of tea which she replenished regularly for the duration of my visit.

Mary was delighted that I was there and that I had asked her to share her stories with me. She loved sharing her tales, and I loved to listen.

We sat there for two and a half hours, during which we laughed, and she cackled as she relayed various incidents to me. It was a wonderful experience. Even though she was so sick, I saw her come alive as she told these tales. Some were funny and some were sad, but she was happy being in amongst those memories, reliving each moment with me.

I hadn't realised how long I was there, and I suddenly saw her fading. I checked the time. "Oh, Mary, I'm so sorry," I said. "I didn't mean to be here this long."

She replied, "I didn't realise either, Val, but I have loved every minute of it. Thank you."

I gently hugged her frail body. I could feel the love emanating from her and knew that today had been a very special day. I didn't want it to end and wanted that hug to last forever.

Mary had prepared well for her own funeral, which wasn't a surprise because she'd always been organised. She had shown me before I left a little brown suitcase, and in it were lists of who should have what from her personal possessions.

There was also a list of the songs, prayers, and readings that would be part of her funeral service. The names of the readers, what readings. My name was there, too, as she had asked me to read a passage from Silver Birch.

My assumption was that when the time came, I would pass this all on to the minister conducting the service; it certainly hadn't occurred to me that I would be the one doing the service.

She didn't want to people to be stressing over all this when she had passed; such was the kindness of Mary.

She was such a dear lady and always wanted to share with others. Over the years she had prepared for church the weekly readings, which were taken from the teachings of Silver Birch. She loved Silver Birch.

Before I left her that last day, she handed me a folder, saying, "I hope you can use this in the future, Val." I felt overwhelmed. It was a copy of each of the Silver Birch teachings. I knew how much work she had put into this and felt very honoured indeed.

I didn't realise that would be our last meeting. All I know is it was special, and it will live in my heart forever.

Back to her daughter's call on the day of her passing and to the funeral service arrangements. I asked her daughter, "Will you be preparing the eulogy?"

"What's one of them?" she asked.

Oh, dear, I was going to be doing everything, but I did know that Spirit and Mary would help me.

How thankful I was that I had spent that time with Mary before she passed because there on that recording was everything I would need to prepare her eulogy.

Every step of this continued journey with Mary was already mapped out. She and Spirit had it all in hand and I was now privy to this. I was astounded and ever so grateful.

I went back to the tape I had recorded and listened to the whole thing. It was lovely to relive that afternoon with Mary. As I worked my way through it, I made notes to prepare the eulogy.

After many hours, I finally finished. I emailed the finished document to her daughter. She got straight on the phone with me.

"Oh, Val, this is wonderful, and it's exactly Mum."

I had been doing my research in the background and knew that we would need an order of service. I asked her, "Have you prepared an order of service?"

"What's that?" she said.

Oh dear, another job I must do, I thought. I didn't mind at all, it was only the sheer amount of organising and the desire to do it as well as I could, in her honour.

Her daughter sent me a beautiful photo of Mary and I put together the order of service with the help of the crematorium staff. I got her daughter's approval as I went along. Mary had, as I have mentioned, chosen songs and readings.

On the day of the actual funeral, the sun shone. It was a stunning English summer's day.

Something was niggling at the back of my mind and then a thought occurred to me: *Who is going to press the button?* Oh nooo.

I rang the crematorium straight away and asked the question. The lovely lady at the other end said, "As the minister for the service, that is your job."

She also reminded me, "Remember you have to keep to time, 30 minutes only, as we have back-to-back services today."

Wow, this is going to be a big, big day; will I cope? I don't want to let Mary or her family down.

I arrived at the crematorium in my favourite cornflower blue dress. Mary's instructions asked everyone was to wear bright colours.

I made my way to the beautiful rose gardens and sat quietly on my own in the sunshine, gathering my thoughts and calming my frazzled nerves.

It was very peaceful as I sat there, and just what I needed.

I recognised various people as they arrived. I then made my way into the crematorium and found my place at the front podium. I was shaking with trepidation of what family and friends would think of me.

People started to file into the crematorium, and as per Mary's instructions, they were all dressed in glorious colours, even the men with their shirts; it was stunning. There was standing room only that day.

The service went off without a hitch. There was much fun and laughter throughout the service and of course the eulogy, which was what Mary would have wanted. All the information from the time spent with Mary sharing her various funny stories.

I felt very proud of myself, and I knew that Mary and Spirit were there, making sure there were no issues. But it was not over yet.

Then came the time to push the button to lower the coffin. My legs went to jelly and tears welled up in my eyes. *Come on, Val, pull yourself together*, I told myself and very quickly regained my equilibrium. I had to do this for Mary.

At the very end of the service, the last song Mary had chosen was 'We'll meet again', by Dame Vera Lynne.

When the music started, the audience just sat quietly, staring. I don't know what made me say it, but I spoke confidently into the microphone and said, "Mary would love it if we all sang along to this song."

I started to sing as loud as I could, and slowly, one by one they all joined in. We raised the roof that afternoon. It was such a glorious moment.

Then as we were singing that song, one of her sons came up from where he was sitting and started pointing to the ceiling and walls.

What is happening? I thought.

I followed his pointing finger, and there on the wall was a ball of golden light dancing up and down the walls. It was also bouncing off people's hymn sheets. *What is that?* I had never seen anything like this before. *Is there a meaning to this?*

The music finished, the room buzzing with excitement and people's chatter. It felt truly magical.

The service was finished. I had done it. The feeling of relief that washed over me was unbelievable.

Then Mary's daughter came bounding up to me and said, "Oh, Val, I don't feel I have been to my mum's funeral; I feel like I've just come out of the theatre. Mum would have loved it."

Afterwards, I walked with the family to where Mary was going to be interred. It was very pretty out in the gardens.

People followed along behind us and kept coming up to me asking if they could put my name down for their own funeral services with comments like: "was the best funeral I've been to", or "it was funny and very personal", or "I'm putting you down to do my funeral service".

We eventually got back to Mary's church for the wake. It's only a small hall and there were many lovely people there, most of whom I knew. After the tea and sandwiches were handed out, her son came up and spoke to me. "Did you see the golden ball of light?"

I nodded and asked, "What was it?"

He then told me how he and Mum had made a pact before she passed about the way she was going to let him know she was still around in Spirit form. He said, "She is amazing. I didn't think she would be able to do it this quickly after her passing."

He went on, "Only she and I knew about this. It was our secret, and we had decided that it was to be a golden ball of light."

Spirit show us in many ways that they are there and that they can certainly help us. Death is not the end, and this sort of communication is the ultimate proof. They verbalised this pact between themselves before she passed; Spirit must have been listening in, too.

Mary would have moved mountains to make this happen; that's the sort of strong special lady she was.

Also, I know that Spirit would have had a part to play in my meeting up with Mary before she died. They knew that had to happen for me to get the information I needed for her funeral service. This was the right place at the right time. Miraculous.

The folder Mary had given me all those years ago with her teachings from Silver Birch had a butterfly that she had stuck onto the front cover. Sadly, over time it became very fragile, and only yesterday I had to repair it. I didn't want to lose it altogether.

As I have been sitting here today writing, there has been a butterfly sitting on my window. It has not moved all day. I would like to think that Mary has been watching over my shoulder making sure I got the details of her story correct. She would be very proud. I love you, Mary.

CHAPTER 13

Other Ways Spirit Can Help Us

I know from many accounts I have read, and experiences people have shared, that we do not just disappear. Our physical body is made up of an energy mass, and according to Einstein, energy cannot be destroyed. Therefore, our physical body passes and the energy of us moves to a different vibration. In the dimension in which we currently exist, there are many levels/dimensions, which means we are not the only ones who inhabit this space.

This is not scary at all; it is very comforting if you look at it in the right way.

The Spirit world work with us always; they don't miss an opportunity and are only too happy to help us when and where they can.

There are various ways to work with Spirit. This can be using mediumship or psychic abilities.

Personally, I like to work mainly with my mediumship skills, which means I am talking and listening to Spirit.

Working in a psychic way, you are using the energies around a person or an object to sense information.

Everything we touch automatically has our energy stamped on it. Whether that is a coin, piece of paper, or, in this case, a cash box!

~❖~

A lady arrived at my door clutching a carrier bag. I had never met her, and I asked her "Where did you get my name?"

She replied, "You came highly recommended by a friend. I have some issues going on at work but can't be sure that I am right in my assumptions. I need some extra help."

We sat down and I asked, as I always do, why she needed a reading. Some people come to connect to a loved one, while others want to know what is going on in their lives.

At this point she shoved the plastic bag into my lap and said, "Can you read this?"

She was asking me to do a psychic reading, to feel the energy of this item, to see if I could pick anything up from it.

I was instantly uncomfortable as I don't really like to do physic readings, or at least I didn't at the time. Mediumship for me is much easier.

I was sitting there with this object in a bag on my lap, which was quite bulky and heavy.

I opened the bag and there was a silver cash box inside, about 12" x 4" x 8".

I was a bit taken aback when she asked me, "Can you read the box, please? What do you pick up about the box?"

I asked for all the help I could muster from the Spirit world. Even though this was a psychic reading and not a mediumship reading, I knew that Spirit was around me and I asked for their help with using my psychic abilities.

I was surprised and astounded as the information started flowing.

I was being shown, in my mind, the most vivid pictures. It was like watching a TV screen going off in my head. I paid close attention to what I was seeing and relayed the information to my client.

"There has been money taken from this box," I said. The lady sat there, stunned. I gave her the amounts taken. "There were two people involved here and you suspect both of them – you know who they are, don't you?" I continued, "I have these initials..."

"Yes, that's correct," she replied.

"I am also being shown that the tin has three hiding places," I told her, and went on to describe them.

She was delighted. "Everything you have told me confirms my suspicions, and yes, I knew they were the people who were responsible."

She left my house happy, as was I, that Spirit had worked with me so well. Even though I was not comfortable doing the psychometry, Spirit had helped me to make this happen for the lady who needed this help.

I know mediums who have been used in murder investigations, one of my old teachers being one. She helped by working on a very big overseas case.

If people were more aware of Spirit being around them, maybe they would think twice before committing a crime. Sadly, though, not everyone believes that Spirit are around us.

This cash box reading did really help the recipient.

The question for me now is, do I act on everything that Spirit tells me?

My answer to this would be yes. However, I would have to be really clear that it is Spirit communicating the information to me and my mind. There is a fine line here. But those of us who work that closely with Spirit will know.

On my first trip to Australia, I was visiting the many family members I had in Australia with my mum and my daughter, which was so exciting for me and a treat for my 40th birthday.

When I was at my Aunty Lynne and Uncle John's for a few days, we were all sitting around, chatting – Mum to my aunt and me to my uncle.

Uncle John suddenly started to cry. He had had several strokes before our visit and had lost his ability to speak. Aunty Lynne was the only one at the time who could understand what he was saying.

She was busy talking to my mum in another room and I called out to her, "Why is Uncle John crying?"

Aunty Lynne came into the room and said, "What's up, John?" She listened, and then started to relay the story to me, "He keeps going on about the blue lights he keeps seeing. He has been dreaming about them for ages. He sees these blue lights and gold stars and has also been seeing a face. He has just realised the face he's been seeing is yours!"

Uncle John had not physically seen me since I was about 8, which was when they left for Australia.

My aunt asked, "Do you understand this at all?"

I smiled at them both and said, "I had heard on the family grapevine that Uncle John was ill and have been sending healing energies to you all that time." I continued, "The blue lights you are seeing will be the healing rays I have been visualising."

They were both really surprised by this, but they were also very happy that I had been sending healing energies to help him.

I tried to explain how healing works and that the absent / distant healing can be done from anywhere. It had obviously been working; how else would Uncle John have been seeing these visions? Spirit are so clever.

Not long after our visit to Australia my uncle passed away.

Then one day, out of the blue, I was back in the UK and got a phone call from my aunt.

I was delighted to hear from her, obviously, and asked how she was and why was she calling.

She said, "Are you still sending those blue lights over here?"

I smiled to myself and replied, "Of course I am; as you have lost Uncle John and are now grieving, you need some healing for yourself. Why do you ask?"

She started to tell me, "Well, I have John's ashes in an urn in the wardrobe and every night blue lights are coming out of the cupboard."

I smiled to myself and told her, "Well, the healing energies I am sending to you are working, then."

We both laughed, and she was happy to accept that it was healing coming all the way from the UK to Australia and she had recognised it as being similar to what my uncle had experienced.

CHAPTER 14

How a Reading Is Healing

When I first came into the spiritualist church, I was enthralled by all things spiritual and the mechanics of mediumship. It was all fascinating, but then there was the healing side of this work.

I had started off as a healer, but after two years I found out that I could not and was not allowed to mix mediumship and healing. I look back now and think that was a very wrong decision that was made for me. But it took me in different directions with my work that I don't regret.

There are many stories of hands-on healing in our modern-day spiritualism and, as I was to learn within my training, many stories in the Bible relating to hands on and distant healing.

Absent/distant healing is sending out healing with a thought. Putting a name in a book with the intention of the healing going to that name.

Hands-on healing is just that. I will describe this below.

I went along to many of the sessions myself. I wanted to witness what happens and to experience this healing for myself. At the time I certainly needed it.

I had lots of questions in the early days: How did it happen? What would I experience? Did it work?

Now, after many years of practicing mediumship and healing, I realise that spiritual healing works on very many levels and in many ways. I have witnessed many such occurrences of how people have been affected physically and emotionally by this healing. It is such a beautiful thing to witness.

I went along one Tuesday afternoon to the healing session at our church. The layout of the church was different from Sunday service. The seating area had been removed and about 12 single seats were spread out in that area instead. This space had been set up for people to receive healing. They called them the healing stations.

Then, at the back of the church, was a single row. This was for people waiting to receive healing.

The feel of the church was different from a Sunday service, too. Sunday service had its chairs laid out in rows from front to back, brightly lit with lively music to lift the energies in the room.

Today, for the healing, the lights were dimmed, with calming healing/meditation music playing in the background. This created a wonderful, serene, peaceful atmosphere.

When I entered, I was greeted by one of the stewards of the church. They asked, "Do you need healing today?"

"Yes, please," I replied.

I was directed to sit in the row of seats at the back of the church. I sat expectantly, and a little nervously; this was the first healing session I had experienced for myself.

As people entered for their healing, I noted they were from all walks of life – male, female, and varying cultures. This surprised me initially. But we were all treated exactly the same, no questions asked. Our details were taken for the church records. This was a protocol required by law.

I sat down along with quite a few other people, surprised by how many people turned up for the healing.

At the front of the church, two healers stood side by side at each of the healing stations. It appeared that they were the older, more experienced members of our church. I found out later they had been healers for many years.

There is a two-year training course with the Federation of Spiritual Healers in the UK. This is their description of spiritual healing:

Spiritual healing is a completely natural process. It is thought to establish a flow of beneficial energy between the healer and the recipient that addresses the 'dis-ease' manifesting at its deepest level, thus seeking to awaken the body's natural resources to work in the most effective way to restore balance, harmony, and wellbeing. Spiritual healing is termed holistic – meaning 'whole' – which means that instead of addressing symptoms in isolation spiritual healing looks to encompass physical, mental, and emotional 'dis-ease'. It views all illnesses as being interlinked and the result of underlying issues of the whole person – the body, mind, and soul.

My name was called, and I was directed to one of the healer stations. I was then asked by a lovely man, "Why are you here today, and how do you think we can help you?"

"I have various issues going on within my body, but also I am an emotional mess," I replied.

"Okay," he said. "We want you to relax. This will be a three-way process: the healer, the patient, and undoubtedly Spirit." He continued, "You may get some sensations in your body when we start; you may feel hot or cold. Whatever you sense, please know that this is perfectly normal." His voice calm, he added, "We want you to enjoy this time and relaxing makes it easier to do this."

I was fascinated to watch as the healers started by putting their hand on my shoulders for a few minutes. After this they did not touch my body. Their hands were held approximately three inches above my skin.

Then, as if directed by some unknown force, they moved to parts of my body they sensed to be problem areas. They were in the right places every time. The heat from their hands was extremely intense. Sometimes, even though there were only two of them working with me, it felt like I had many other pairs of hands on my body.

Suddenly, one of them stopped over my lungs, and it felt like a 'hot rod' going through my body. It felt truly amazing.

When they had finished, the lady healer spoke. "You have had problems with your lungs."

"Yes," I replied.

How do they know that? I was quite ill at the time, not outwardly obvious, but I had severe lung issues that had hospitalised me several times. And so, it went on – every time they stopped in a certain area of my body, that was where I had a problem.

When they had finished, I felt very different. It was as if a surge of energy had passed through my body. I could not believe this feeling. I felt lighter, as if the pain was being lifted and the issues within my body were minimised, if not being removed. Week after week, I could feel the difference this healing was making to me physically, mentally, and emotionally.

When I felt a lot better in myself, I inquired as to whether I could join the healer training programme myself.

I was interviewed by the president of the church, who was also a NFSH healer and examiner. She said, "There are a few other suitable candidates, and we are, therefore, almost ready to go with a new course and we would love to have you on it."

You had to be a part of the church for a certain period of time. This gave the church the opportunity to know a little about you. You had to be interested in spiritual matters, and of course healing, as this work would take dedication and commitment.

At the time, I was a part of everything at our church; I was, therefore, seen as qualified to start the training.

They gave a complete breakdown of what would be required of us as trainees, and we had to agree to all this. We would also have to attend other churches as well as our own for assessment.

This felt exciting, and I was full of anticipation for what was to come. I would be working with my spiritual team of healing guides. *Why wouldn't I be excited?*

I was anxious to meet the team. All the trainees were feeling a little nervous.

We were to practice amongst the healing group initially. We all took it in turns to be the healer or the patient.

Our teacher told us, "We are going to be transferring energy from the Spirit world, through the Spirit of the healer, to the Spirit of the recipient. From Spirit, through Spirit, to Spirit."

It all sounded easy; I trusted what I was being told. Our teacher had been a healer herself for over 50 years.

I stood nervously, awaiting my turn to be the healer. When the time came, I stretched out my hands, as I had seen the other healers do, gently touched my patient's shoulders, and waited for something to happen.

Our teacher said, "Ask your healing Spirit guides to step forward to help you."

I did as she asked. By this time, I was used to asking Spirit for help, and this seemed like a very natural process.

Then, to my utter amazement, it felt as if my body was growing and changing and shaking. My arms were growing longer, and I could feel my body becoming taller. It was like I was becoming someone else. This was a bit alarming to start with.

My teacher could see my alarm. "Don't block it. Allow the process to happen and the energies to flow through you. You are being joined by your healing guide, who was a doctor when he was here on earth."

I calmed myself and just went with the flow as she directed.

I was fascinated that she could see this Spirit man, too.

I felt my Spirit doctor step back and knew that the healing was finished. I then spoke to the patient and explained what I had picked up regarding their health. They gave their responses.

"Thank you for that feedback that fills me with the confidence to keep doing the healing work," I said.

I continued my training, having many memorable experiences. But as I was coming to the end of my two years, I had an experience that would change the direction of my spiritual work.

An older man came to me one day for his healing. He looked very forlorn and thin, wearing a dirty old raincoat, and was unshaven. He looked like he could do with a good hearty meal.

"Hello," I said. "How can I help you? Have you had healing before?"

He replied, "No, I have not been here before. I just lost my wife recently."

I started to give him healing and was very aware of an older lady from Spirit standing with him. She told me, "I am his wife."

I knew that this was a healing session and not meant for messages. We were taught at the time that we had to keep these two things separate. You were either doing healing or messages, not both at the same time.

Therefore, I didn't pass on the information she was giving. She continued, "I have only recently passed, and my husband is not looking after himself. I want to tell him I love him and am still with him."

It made me feel unhappy that I could not pass this information on to him. But I had to follow the rules. I even spoke to my teacher about this after our session, and she said that I was not allowed to pass on any messages during healing.

Passing on information from a Spirit doctor was okay, but if a loved one was to step forward, we could not share that.

This was my defining moment. For me, anything to do with Spirit should be about healing. To be told that I could not pass on such wonderful messages to help the grieving was criminal, I thought.

If I had been able to share with that old man the information from his wife, what a difference that could have made to him.

I know that this lovely man did get spiritual healing from this session, and from his newly departed wife.

What I didn't like was watching a really unhappy man walk out of our church without receiving that comfort and upliftment I thought he was deserving of.

I feel that if he had received a message letting him know that his wife was there with him, it would have made a world of difference to him.

I could not continue with my healing training after this, as this did not seem fair to me. I therefore decided to concentrate solely on my mediumship, which I knew would bring healing from the wonderful messages shared from Spirit.

Over the years I have been doing this work, I have seen so much healing come from a reading. I will always make sure that a person leaves me feeling the love and warmth of the loved ones gathered around them.

As well as the hands-on healing, there is absent healing. This is where you send your thoughts out to the Spirit world, asking them to direct healing towards the person, persons, group, or world you want the healing power to go to. The power of collective healing is very special, and I have seen this work.

In the many churches and centres I have worked in across the world, there are healing books. In this book, you can enter the name of a person/s or animal or a country. The centres throughout the week will pray upon the book, and again, collectively thoughts go out to these people from all participants of that centre. Many of us underestimate the power of collective thought and prayer; it is a very powerful way of making things happen and seeing very powerful results.

During the time I was training, I read many books on the subject of spiritualism and healing. Some of my favourite books that became my bibles included a trilogy by the late Betty Shine, who was a brilliant medium and healer herself. I tapped into her knowledge constantly. It was simple but effective.

One day, I was on the early morning train on my way to work in London, reading one of these books. In it she described how you could do distant healing.

She described using your mind's eye and imagining a beautiful blue laser beam of light. Once you formulated this beam in your mind, you just aimed it where it was needed. This sounded pretty exciting to me, so I thought I would give it a go.

The train was pulling into Victoria Station in London, and as I closed the book, I looked up and could not believe my eyes. There in front of me, leaning against the wall of the train, was a young man on crutches and his leg in plaster. *Perfect opportunity, not to be missed*, I thought. *I have got to try this.*

I imagined, as Betty had suggested, this beautiful laser beam of light, and zapped the young man with it. Oh, my goodness, I could not believe what happened next, this poor fellow fell over.

Is it me? Is it that powerful? Did anyone see me do that?

I was not hanging around to find out. I ran incredibly fast off that train. I have laughed about this so many times since. It may have been a coincidence or not! However, I was hoping that my laser beam was THAT powerful. Another magical moment with Spirit.

I have used this technique many times since but not had such dramatic results.

Having a reading is extremely healing. People come for many reasons – the loss of a loved one, direction, questions, plus so much more. It never ceases to amaze me, the appearance or behaviour of a person when they arrive for their reading compared to how they leave. This is very contrasting. They can arrive sad, distraught, nervous, crumpled, and leave ten feet taller, happy, their whole energy changed, and their Spirit visibly lifted.

There are some, however, who you will never be able to help. They will block their energies before you start, with a sceptical 'prove it to me attitude', or they just don't believe.

I personally don't understand why these people come for a reading in the first place. If you do come for a reading, then come with an open mind. That is all that is expected of you.

I love doing readings for those who need to connect to a loved one. This allows me to make those links, bringing through the personality and mannerisms of the Spirit loved one.

Those who want a generalised psychic reading and don't want to connect to a loved one, I find more difficult to do. It feels I am being tested in some way.

There is a place for both a psychic and spiritual reading. The need of the reader must be met.

There are some people who have too many readings. They practically want the Spirit world to run their lives for them.

I try to help those people to understand that we have our physical lives, and we have a personal responsibility to live our lives the best way we can. It is our own responsibility, not that of the Spirit world. They can guide us and help us where they can, but they cannot do it for us.

These are a few examples of how a reading can help to change your lives.

I had three young ladies who came to me for a reading within a six-month period. One was bulimic, one anorexic, and one suicidal. For me this was quite surprising, to have three in six months.

They each had their readings, and each received love, guidance, and support from the other side. As a result of that communication from Spirit, each of them went away uplifted. They are all still alive today and are happy and healthy.

What Spirit had done was to point out to them how special their life was in as many ways they could. They told these women what wonderful and exciting things they had in front of them. This helped to change their outlook on life and give them hope, upliftment, motivation, and much more. A reason to live.

I became very good friends with one of these ladies. Her life turned around in such an incredible way, and this was possible because of the words that came from her relatives in Spirit.

The information that came through may have appeared to others to be just little things but were to her insurmountable. Spirit helped her overcome many obstacles that had faced her for many years.

Now I see this beautiful young lady, having grown in so many ways, and she is happy and healthy. She didn't think any of these things were possible all those years ago.

One day a tall, elegant, beautiful lady walked into my home for her reading, but the feel of her energy told me she was very unhappy.

I started her reading, and her dad came through showing love and joy. He gave her incredible detail of himself in order to prove that it was really her dad I was connecting to.

"This is the first time my dad has come through since his passing," she told me.

She was overwhelmed, and I could see a visible change in her straight away. She started to beam and glow. By the end of the reading, it was like I had a different person with me. She was happy and laughing and her energy had grown and visibly changed. I could physically see the change in her.

When I had finished the reading, she explained to me, "I was diagnosed with cancer and have been seriously ill. I have not been coping at all." She continued, "I'll be leaving my two young boys behind without a mum, without me!"

With a sad sigh, she said, "I've just been sitting for weeks in my dressing gown, not going out, or doing any normal things with my family. Up to this point I'd given up. I didn't see the point of life if I was going to die. But today, this reading has changed that."

Sobbing, she said, "My dad being here today has proved to me there is more to life, and while I'm here, I have to live it the best way I can for my boys and for me."

She left a completely different woman. I didn't think I would see or hear from her again.

However, about two weeks later I received a parcel in the post, which I wasn't expecting. I opened it and was extremely surprised when I looked inside the box. There was a stone circle of friends and a card. It was from this young lady. The card read:

I have spent over two years terrified of my cancer and the voices in my head. One hour with you and everything fell into place. I feel safe, in control, and ALIVE!! You have given me my life back and helped me escape from the saddest place in the universe. I shall be eternally grateful, and whether you want one or not, you have acquired a true friend for life!! Thank you – you have given back my boys their mum and my husband his wife. How cool is that!!? You will always have a special place in my heart. I can't thank you enough.

That gift and card I still treasure and have pride of place to this day.

I was lucky to have shared some of that extra time she had, as we became very good friends. More importantly, she got to spend two happy extra years with her family. She lived that to the best she could. Making memories for all of them.

That's the magic of a spiritual reading for a lot of people. It can be life changing.

I had the privilege of going to her funeral, and when I listened to the words spoken at her service from family and friends, they spoke of the change in her during her last two years.

The loss of a child have been, for me, some of the hardest readings to deal with. I have three of my own and I cannot fathom the pain and loss that would go with losing any of them.

However, there was a period of four months where many of the readings I did regarded the loss of a child. This coincided with each of my children dealing with an illness and not knowing what the outcome of this would be.

I got scared that Spirit was preparing me for something. I was not sure. I asked Spirit what was going on.

They explained: "*We have loved ones in our lives for a certain period of time. During that time, we have to cherish them, make the most of every minute, of every experience.*"

I took on board what I was told, and I got on with savouring every moment of life.

I hope as you read these accounts that you will feel the love and the healing that have taken place. All readings are special and meaningful.

I was at a church in Farnham in the UK when I was still quite new at doing spiritualist church services. I sat nervously alongside the chairperson, who was quite unfriendly, which didn't help my nerves. In her defence, we can't all be chatty, and maybe she was coping with her own nerves on the day, as she was the chairperson. Who knows?

The audience was quite large and growing by the minute.

I started to do my readings and made the most wonderful connection for a mum. I will share what she wrote to me, as it says it better than I can. This is one of those experiences I will never forget.

I was at the spiritualist church in Farnham last Sunday with my mum and my partner Geoff. I have always believed in the afterlife and discussed it freely with my boys, Kieran had even attended with me a few times. I had stopped going – not needing the reassurance that it brings until both my boys died. Last Sunday my babies had been gone for 8 weeks only. The medium arrived. Her name was Val Hood; she had never been to the Farnham church before. She said she had a message from a young man who had died tragically and recently and proceeded to describe my 9-year-old – she then stopped, and with tears in her eyes, said that his sibling was with him and described my 11-year-old. Now I know from visiting this website that losing two children is very rare – you wouldn't make it up. She then went on to tell me about many things that I have and haven't been doing that she would never have known. She also came up to me afterwards and apologised for not being able to produce their names – trust me, I didn't mind, my partner, my mother, and I were all in tears – Geoff has said that it's the most amazing experience of his life. It has lifted my Spirits so much, to lose both my boys has totally devastated my life but this one woman has given me such hope.

It is sad enough to lose one child, but both of them together like this is unfathomable. The love, emotion, and joy that came from this reading that afternoon I remember really well, like it was yesterday.

These people had been sitting solemnly in the audience. I had no idea who they were; I did not live in their area, and I had driven a fair distance to be at the church that day.

However, seeing the happiness on the faces of this family as the boys connected was pure joy for me.

This is something I see often, and I do feel blessed and honoured to do this work, making those incredible connections from Spirit to lift the Spirits of those left behind.

Another experience I had was at a book launch/conference with a wonderful author/friend, Barry Eaton. This was in Buderim, Queensland.

The event was set up as a high tea. It was beautifully set out with exquisite fine bone china and high tiered trays covered in delicious cakes, sandwiches, and chocolates.

There were about 40 people enjoying this glorious setting and food. After the book launch and talk by Barry, I was asked to do a mediumship demonstration. The following day I was to do a workshop.

~❖~

I was introduced, and I explained to the audience who I was and a little bit about my background.

I started to work with Spirit, making link after link to very happy people in the audience. Bringing their loved ones through.

In the middle of my demonstration, I was drawn to an older lady. "I have a young man here for you," I said. "He tells me he is your son, and he passed a long time ago."

I went on to bring such valuable evidence through, including how he had died. Very emotionally, she accepted everything I gave her. Tears flowed down her face.

I said, "He tells me he is sorry for his passing, and he is pulling on a beanie."

The rest of the event passed, and I did not get a chance to talk to this lady; although she was nodding in the affirmative all the way through, she could not talk through her tears.

However, a few days later I got this email:

My Aunt Val in Queensland attended a dinner book launch of "On the Other Side", and you spoke to her about her son Robert who died by suicide over 20 years ago. She has asked me to thank you as, on the day of your event, she was in shock, and it took a while for the experience to sink in. She said he always wore the beanies.

You told her that he is now trying to look after people who are contemplating suicide. I am a bereavement counsellor and I wish to thank you for the support you gave Val. It is so encouraging to see how people can be supported/assisted by meeting with mediums. After the horrific bushfires in Victoria some years back, one of the senior psychologists I work with said that attending psychics really helped those who had become stuck on the horror of how their loved ones had died. Thank you for all the good work. God Bless. Sunshine Coast Qld.

Readings bring healing in many wonderfully different ways. This reading was very different but nonetheless healing. A very different experience for me.

A lot of people come for readings wanting you to tell them what they WANT to hear NOT what they NEED to hear. This was one of those readings!

A strait-laced lady came into my home, looking fraught and restrained. She was quiet and not overly friendly. As she settled herself down on my lovely cream sofa and I prepared my recording machine, I heard a voice in my head telling me, "She wants you to tell her it's okay to leave her husband".

I thought to myself, *oh, this is going to be interesting.* Then the little voice, that of a lady, told me, "*But we are not going to tell her that.*"

Uh oh. What was going to happen here?

I got on with what I was supposed to be doing and made that gorgeous connection with the loved one who had been 'in my ear', and she just happened to be the lady's nan.

She brought through the evidence of herself and the type of relationship she had with her granddaughter.

This confirmation of who we are talking to is important. We need to know who is giving the information to us. This is what evidential mediumship is about.

Nan gave her granddaughter information about what was going on with the granddaughter's marriage. Nan told her she was certainly NOT to give up on it, and then proceeded to tell her the very many ways that she could make this work.

My client was not happy at all. Reluctantly, she gave me my money and left.

I did not expect to hear from her again, but I did a year later!

I got an email from her: "You will probably not remember me, but I came for a reading a year ago and wanted to leave my husband, and you told me my nan told me not to".

The email came as a shock. She went on to say, "I need to say thank you, as I listened and took on board what my nan had said, and I now have the best marriage ever, thank you."

These readings really do have a great way of working their magic. I bet her nan would have been the same type of strong, verbal person when she was alive, getting her point across in a very determined way. I love that this can, firstly, prove the person we are connecting to and, secondly, that their help is invaluable. Thank you, Nan.

All readings, no matter what they are for – whether direction, or connection to loved ones – are very powerful, and the healing is incredibly tangible. Magic happens!

CHAPTER 15

Child Experiences of Spirit

Many children see Spirit, and like me as a child, it must be very frustrating and frightening when these things happen. From my own experience and the vast number of stories I have heard, Spirits are around children until about the age of 8. This is when the big bad world takes over and that innocent ability to be able to see is taken away.

Often children are stopped from seeing Spirit for various reasons. Parents who don't understand, or think their children are making it up or have imaginary friends, or the parents themselves have a fear of the unknown and don't want to know or to learn about such things.

Do you remember having experiences as a child, or with your own children? Have they been chatting away and there is no one there? Do they mention the man in the corner or someone's playing with their toys?

We should pay more attention, as there are more children who talk to Spirit than we are aware of.

Spirit love kids; children are playful and usually not scared of them, and in the main it's a family member who wants to play as Spirit would have done if they were still physically here. In the main, though, Spirit loves the innocence of children and their tendency to not question.

As I have already mentioned, my own experiences of seeing dead people, like my Nana, was very scary indeed. But I had nobody to talk to about it at the time. I personally thought my family would think I was a nutter. This is very common with kids. They are frightened of what people will think of them if they mention these things.

I would like to tell you of my own children and their experiences, which were quite interesting and funny.

Neil, my eldest, was the first to see Spirit. We lived in a little cul-de-sac in a small Welsh village. I tried hard to keep the boys in the confines of our garden, but they always found a way out. I gave up in the end as it was a quiet, safe street and there was no real danger for our kids to play out in the street. Our house was right on top of this cul-de-sac, and I could see where they were most of the time.

It was a beautiful summer's day in July, and as it was school holidays, trying to keep the boys entertained was challenging. They were 4 and 3, very much a handful, always getting up to some mischief or other. There were a couple of other kids out there with them that day. They all descended upon me when their bellies were rumbling, and they knew I would feed them. They were all constantly hungry. They popped in and out often, the whole group of them.

Neil was sitting nibbling away at his goodies with one of his besties by his side on the doorstep to the kitchen. I was in the kitchen busying myself. I could see them and hear their conversation very clearly.

Suddenly Neil said to his friend, "I have a lady who visits me at night-time." He continued, "She comes from the light in my bedroom ceiling."

That made my ears prick up I can tell you. He carried on, "She is so lovely and pretty and holds my hand and talks to me."

Was this what I thought it was? Was he really seeing something, or was this just a 4-year-old's imagination playing out here? I would have to keep an eye on this situation.

Later that day I went to see my mum and told her what had happened. She told me, "He is either making it up, hallucinating, or it is real. Leave it a while and see if he mentions it again."

Well, me being me, I couldn't leave it there. I was intrigued to know what was going on. I didn't want any of my children to go through what I had as a child. I wanted them to know they could talk to me about such things, and that I would understand.

When we got home, I carefully asked him, "I heard you talking to John about the lady coming from the light in your ceiling. You were talking about her today? Do you know who she is?"

He said, "I don't know, Mummy." He followed on with, "But she won't hurt me; she just holds my hand and talks to me."

I asked him if he could describe the lady. I didn't prompt him. I couldn't believe what I was hearing.

He told me, "She has red hair with white in it and she wears an orange dress. She has a very kind smiley face and asks me all about me. She comes from the light in my ceiling in my bedroom."

Was I surprised or not? My little boy was describing MY Nana who died when I was 7 years old. He was seeing her the same way I had – the hair, the white streak, the colour of her clothes.

I explained to him that she would not harm him, and he replied, "I know that, Mummy." However, after this sighting he had to sleep with the light on in the hallway every night. A bit of reassurance, I suppose, and I don't blame him.

Many years later, as a grown man with children of his own, he is now a singer–songwriter. He writes many songs, and I just go in and listen to them as they come up. But this day I was overwhelmed when listening to this latest song. He was publicly declaring to the world in song about his experience of seeing my Nana.

It was so beautiful, and the day I heard this song, it brought tears to my eyes to listen to him sharing that experience in this way.

Close to Me by Neil J Fraser

When I was a boy a long time ago
I woke one night from a dream
The moon shone brightly my brother asleep
And no sign of what I had just seen
As I lay down my heart beating fast
Hoping sleep would close my eyes
I saw above me a flicker of light
Then a lady appeared at my side
CHORUS
As I travel this life, I remember the night
It gives me the comfort I need
No matter what trouble I find on the way
There is always someone standing close to me
She held my hand and said not a word
As I could only stare
Her complexion was clear, her eyes like stars
With the sun red glow of her hair
I shook with fear as I'd never known
As I stared into her eyes
And all the while she quietly stood
With her hand on mine and a smile
When I was calm and frightened no more
The lady I no longer saw
Only my darkened room the pale moon outside
And my brother asleep as before
I ran out to my parent's room
And spoke of what I had just seen
They listened to the tale of a child
That could not have been more than a dream

My second child, Gareth, has big issues with what I do for a living. I have talked to him many times about it, but he is not interested. Both the boys came to the spiritualist church with me many years ago, but they were a bit shocked when the medium stood up and did a trance demonstration. They laughed about it at the time, but I think that would have been nerves to a certain extent.

The old man, Ron Perry, stood on the platform. He was a very gentle, quiet man. He was a great healer and trance medium. When Spirit came to him in trance and he started to speak, it was in this enormous booming voice that made us all jump out of our seats. It was that loud. All the regulars at the church were used to this, but I forgot to forewarn the boys.

When Ron started to speak, the boys just burst out laughing.

Many years later, Gareth, who is now a scientist, looks at things in a very different way. He is much more analytical. The rest of us are arty and creative.

He moved to America to pursue his career. He was in a lonely situation initially.

One day I got this email from him. "Hi Mum, I need to tell you about something that has happened to me." He went on, "I came home from work one day as I was really sick, feeling homesick and very alone. I went to bed to sleep. A short while later I had to get up to go to the bathroom, and I realised the front door to my apartment was wide open. I got up and shut it, went into the bathroom as planned, came back out and there again, the door was open!"

He went on, "I sat on my bed contemplating what had just happened and as I sat there, the TV switched itself on and off several times."

I was intrigued and immediately rang him. "And what do you think it is?" I asked.

He replied, "Well I am sick, feeling lonely, and homesick, and I presume someone is trying to let me know I am not alone."

I asked him, "Who do you think it is?"

He replied, "Probably Grandad."

His Grandad had not been in Spirit that long, and I agreed that it would probably be him, keeping an eye on Gareth.

"So, are you okay now?" I asked him.

"Yep," was his reply, and that was the end of the conversation. He put the phone down, and it's never been mentioned again since!

He can't deny it happened, though.

Then there was Victoria, my youngest. From the age of 2 she had been seeing and playing with Spirit.

Two of the Spirits around her had names, too. The boy was Boyfriend, and the girl was Lizzie. They were her constant companions. She would have conversations with them all the time. She was not afraid at all.

It was funny when we went to the supermarket, as she would ask, "Please, Mummy, can we have two seats as Boyfriend and Lizzie want to sit with me." Therefore, a two-seater trolley would be collected.

They would come on journeys in the car with us. She found it funny and would say, "Boyfriend is sitting on the dashboard, Mummy; he is so naughty."

Lizzie, however, sat in the seat next to her. "She has to have a seat belt on, Mummy."

I always obliged her by putting Lizzie in the seat belt.

They also came on holidays with us.

One day Victoria told me, "Boyfriend was naughty, Mummy, he didn't listen to his daddy. He told him not to go too far and he did."

She described him living in the country near a forest. The reason his dad told him not to go too far was that there was a pond there and his dad didn't want him near it.

She was even able to describe how he was dressed. "He has a hat on, it's flat, like the one Grandad wears. He also has long shorts with 'things' on holding them up." She then told me, "He went in the water and didn't come out." He had drowned.

Victoria never mentioned Lizzie's story.

Sometimes they were not mentioned for a while and I would ask her, "Where are Boyfriend and Lizzie?"

She replied, "I don't know, probably gone to see their parents, I suppose."

I loved this connection she had to Spirit. She was a total natural.

Many years later, when she was around 13, I asked her again, "Where are Boyfriend and Lizzie? You haven't mentioned them for ages."

Her reply made me giggle, "You know they are here, and I know they are here, so let's leave it there!"

There was another little girl who came only a few times, but she frightened Victoria. She was in our bathroom and used to just pop up.

Victoria was still quite young at the time, and I asked her, "Well, where does she come from?"

Her answer was funny. "Probably the plughole, for all I know!"

I think my kids were lucky that I understood these connections, and I spoke to them about what they were experiencing. I loved to find out who they were connecting to and the Spirit's story.

I wanted them to feel safe and secure and to know that what was happening was the most natural thing in the world. I would have hated to be one of those mums who say it's just an imaginary friend or don't be silly, you're making it up. Especially bearing in mind my own experiences as a young child.

I feel for the kids who get that reaction from their parents. They are supposed to make us feel safe, not stupid.

Can you imagine how a child must feel, when they ARE seeing something, they mention it to their parent, who tells them 'Don't be stupid'.

This ability is the most natural thing in the world. Our loved ones are around us always, looking out for us and protecting us. We need to help our children believe and understand that, too.

One day I was very lucky to spend time with two young boys. Their parents believed in Spirit and had told me of the experiences the boys were having. I said, "I would like to come and chat to them and see what they can tell me, if that would be okay with you."

We agreed on a date and time, and I was very excited to meet up with them.

It was a beautiful experience and one I will never forget. I turned up at their house and was invited in. I was greeted by two very excited little boys.

They obviously knew who I was. Mum and Dad had explained why I was coming and told them that I had special friends just like them.

We sat and had a cup of tea so I could generally chat with the boys to make sure they were comfortable with me. Luckily, there were no worries there; they were very keen to share their stories.

Mum made her excuses and left the three of us together. I just chatted casually at first. "What are your names? How old are you both?" I asked them about school and the things they liked.

Then I said, "Mum tells me that you are able to see Spirit people. Do you want to tell me about them?" Well, they couldn't tell me quickly enough and both at the same time.

At that point I went and sat nearer the boys, and instantly got told off. "You can't sit there, you'll sit on him."

"Oops, I'm sorry." I went and sat elsewhere.

"You nearly sat on magic man," they said.

They then went on to describe who it was that I nearly sat on. "He plays games with us all the time."

It was such a magical afternoon with them. They even stroked a Spirit dog. It was all very real to the boys, and I loved sharing with them.

I told them of the things I saw when I was their ages. They asked lots of questions.

"What did you see?"

"Who were they?"

"Did they scare you?"

"Did they play with you?"

We spent approximately two hours sharing stories. They excitedly pointed out when someone else had come into the room. They described vivid colours, shapes etc. Some of the people they described were very strange looking and had odd colours.

The thing they loved was that I didn't laugh at them, I didn't question what they were seeing; I knew it to be true, and they responded well to me because they needed someone else to believe them, and I did. I loved the fact that they were experiencing similar things to myself. They loved it, too.

One of the stories I loved was they told me they had been shown the Halls of Knowledge. This is a place in the Spirit world that holds all the information about everyone on planet earth who has ever existed.

"There is an enormous book that you can look at that has everyone's story in it," they told me. "The people there don't have faces or feet. They have brown cloaks with hoods, and they just float around."

This was a description that I had heard many times throughout my own learning.

"Do they scare you?" I asked.

"Nooooooo, they are really kind and will help you with anything you need," one of them said.

"The building has lots of floors and if you want to go up or down, you just click your fingers," one of them told me.

"You actually move through the floors, which are like marshmallow," the youngest one told me, "You just float in between." He indicated up and down with his hands as he spoke.

I asked, "Don't you get all sticky?"

"Oh, don't be silly, that doesn't happen," was the reply.

They told me, "There are so many other books and hundreds of bookshelves all around the building. If you want to know anything you just ask one of the men in cloaks and they will tell you where to find what you want."

"They don't talk to you though," said one of the boys. "You just know in your head what they're telling you."

All the time they were telling me the stories, they would suddenly point to the ceiling. "Oh, here is another one come to join us," and many more Spirits joined as the afternoon went on.

They were incredibly happy to share all their stories and friends with me. I didn't want to leave that day, nor did they want me to leave.

I went home, and I don't know who was the most excited, me or them. It was a very memorable, special day.

Another little boy I met, James, had one of those labels I hate, for instance ADD, ADHD. I know that I am not a doctor, but my experiences on meeting some of these labelled children are that not only are they very clever but have probably been here a million times (reincarnation), and as such they know it all. They are also extremely psychic. Therefore, for them normal everyday school will be boring.

James said to me one day, "I hate school 'cos I've already done that, I know it all."

I had this with two of my children, with them being described as disruptive in class. They were both psychic and seeing Spirit.

With my daughter, for instance, I had to pull her out of school and move her to another school that was going to challenge her more. This was the best decision to make and made such a difference to her.

With James, his mum told me about his disruptive behaviour at school and at home. She was at her wit's end as to what to do with him.

I asked her, "Can I talk to him? Does he talk about spiritual stuff also?"

"Yes, he does all the time," she said, "and I would love it if you could talk to him."

She was desperate to try to understand him and prepared to give anything a go.

The day came for me to meet him, and in walked this little blond-haired 8-year-old. Mum went and sat in her car.

"Hi James," I said. "I'm Val. It's lovely to meet you. How old are you, and what are some of your favourite things to do?"

I love kids and therefore find getting them on side very easy.

"I hear you can see Spirit people, is that right?" I asked him.

"Yes, I can," he said, a little timidly.

"Wow, so do I," I said. "Do you want to tell me about the people you see?"

Bingo – it was as if I had said the magic words for him. I had given him permission to speak about all the spooky things that had been happening to him.

"I have been seeing things for a while now and they show themselves to me in different ways," he said. "There is one of them under your carpet right now."

"Can you describe who or what it was?"

"It's a small goblin type thing. He looks funny with pointy ears and a funny nose."

"Why is he under my carpet?"

"He's scared to come out in case you see him. He only wants children to see him."

Then James told me about all the others who came to him at night-time. There were rather a lot of them, apparently.

I asked him, "Are you scared?"

He replied, "No, they won't hurt me; they come to show me things and talk to me. They're my friends."

As he was talking, my attention was drawn to my guitar. I felt that I was being directed by Spirit.

"Do you like music?" I asked.

He replied, "Yes, I do. I am trying to learn the notes."

I asked him to explain what he meant by the notes, and he drew on a piece of paper some musical notes.

When I asked him how he was doing this, he said, "I sneak Mum's phone and learn the notes on there. I want to play the piano."

"Do you have a piano at home?" I asked.

"No," he said. "I'm saving my pocket money to buy one."

My heart melted. This child was remarkably smart and talented and way above his years on so many things.

I had an electric keyboard, and I asked him, "Would you like to borrow this?"

He shyly replied, "I would love that."

When we had finished chatting, I walked him out to Mum's car and asked her, "Would it be okay if I loaned my electric keyboard to him?" She agreed.

That day an excited little boy went home with my keyboard.

Many months later, I bumped into James's mum and asked how he was getting on with his music. She told me he was learning very quickly and loving it. I was thrilled that Spirit had directed me by pointing out an instrument in my home and that I could help him in a small way.

CHAPTER 16

Coincidences, or Are They?

Do you see feathers all the time? Or butterflies? Or rainbows? Why? Is there a reason? Is there something drawing your attention to these things?

Over the years, Spirit has tried many ways to let me know they are there, and most of the time I have probably been going around with my eyes shut really tight, sailing through life oblivious to their presence. Spirit must get a bit fed up with me, and us in general.

I feel they must be knocking us on the head saying, "Hello, are you listening? I am trying to talk to you!"

It is the most natural thing in the world for Spirit to be with us and for them to give us this help.

After all, these wonderful beings in Spirit, who used to be our loved ones or friends, are only trying to say "hello", "we are here", "something is not right", "let me help you", "we need your attention for..."

People I talk to have lots of ways that Spirit let them know they are around. As you'll know from an earlier chapter, feathers were initially my sign. But as time has gone on, there have been many other things they have used. We have to pay close attention, as they don't want us to become complacent and will change things up regularly.

We need to learn to recognise these signs. Maybe you could ask them for a particular sign and see what happens.

I hear a lot of people saying, "Oh, it's just a coincidence that I saw that", but I don't believe in coincidences as far as Spirit is concerned. When they want to show you something, or to get a message across to you, they will try every way possible to do that. It is truly miraculous and something we really should be more aware of.

The Oxford Dictionary describes the word coincidence as meaning "a remarkable concurrence of events or circumstances without apparent causal connection".

I look back on some of my own weird happenings and now say, "Yep, that was them". I always thank them; they are only trying to help us, after all.

What are your coincidences? How have your Spirit loved ones been trying to get your attention?

The coincidences could be:

- You take a wrong road and find out later that the other route was blocked due to a road accident.

- You leave for an appointment five minutes early or late, and again you have avoided an incident.

I have heard many stories of people missing a connection, for instance when travelling, and something really dramatic happens. They were not meant to be there at that time.

Some people may think this is just a coincidence. I don't think they are coincidences; I think Spirit finds a way somehow to let you know they are around.

These are a few of my coincidences, or at least I would like to think they are.

When I was 16, my Grandad had been in a dementia ward for a year or so. He had this illness when Nana died and Mum looked after him for as long as she could, but it got too difficult. He would go out and get lost, give away his pension monies, and had generally deteriorated; it was therefore not safe for him to be at home.

It was Christmas week and Mum was up to her eyes in planning and preparations. You can imagine what that is like for a family of eight. I said I would go and visit Grandad on Christmas Eve and take in his gifts.

When I went in and said hello, he didn't really know who I was.

Once again, I had that eerie feeling, my gut instinct on full alert. *This means that something is not right, but what?*

When I got home, I was chatting to Mum and said, "I don't think Grandad will be with us much longer."

She asked me how I knew that, and I explained, "It's just a feeling that I have, but I know I'm right."

Christmas Day arrived, and my sister and I were excited that after lunch our boyfriends were coming to visit.

It was very odd that day because from about lunchtime, it sounded like the front door was being knocked on. Our front door has a glass panel in it and you could clearly see that there was no one there.

Frustratingly, this happened continually through the next few hours. Then, at 4 pm, again there was a knock at the door. I got annoyed as I thought the boys were playing games with us. I went to the door and even though I could see no one there I opened the door.

Five minutes after I opened the door, our telephone rang. It was the hospital to say that Grandad had in fact died at 4 pm.

We all believed that Grandad had been knocking to come home and when the door was finally opened, he was able to do just that; he had come back to his home.

Now he and Nana were back together again.

After Christmas, my dad had the idea to do a Ouija board session. This was done regularly with his mum when Dad was a young boy.

We set everything up in Grandad's old room, the table with the letters, yes and no, and a glass.

We all sat around the table in readiness. The lights were switched off and candles lit. We would go around the circle, taking it in turns to ask a question. But the question had to be asked silently, so no one would know what question had been asked.

We got started and the name of the person connecting was spelled out: Hilda. Nana was there. Various questions were asked, and we got the right answers. All was going well. It was very exciting and we were all thrilled with the answers to our questions.

Then another question was asked, and the glass spun out of control and flew off the table, shattering glass everywhere.

We all ran in different directions, not knowing what had happened or why.

When we eventually calmed down, Dad asked what question had been asked.

It had in fact been, "Is Grandad with you now?"

We were all pretty freaked out by this, and as it had only been a few days since his passing, did she know, had he not met up with her yet. We had so many questions.

Suffice it to say we didn't do that again.

I know that Grandad is now with Nana as I have had proof of it over the years.

I have in fact done other Ouija board sessions with a local paranormal group, but these were held in controlled situations. I would NOT recommend you do these unless you know what you are doing.

I drove from Surrey to Huntingdon, which was a fairly gruelling two-hour drive. The weather was horrendous; it was lashing down with rain and the roads were laden with traffic. I didn't think I was going to make the show on time.

I arrived very flustered what with the weather and the traffic and I was panicked that I was going to be late, but, by the skin of my teeth, I made it on time. I had arranged to meet up with Bill, who ran his own radio station in the town and had interviewed me on his show to promote my event.

The Commemoration Hall was the venue for my mediumship show. I walked into this majestic building and was stunned by the exquisite foyer with its sweeping wooden staircase and ornate pillars. It was like stepping back in time or onto a film set. We ascended the stairs to find a beautiful old hall, with chairs laid out in readiness for the show. I was excited now. Bill was a funny man, and he had already put me at ease.

Slowly, people started arriving, and with the hum of their voices growing by the minute, I could sense the excitement in the air. This all boded well for a good night.

Eventually all seats had been filled and I was ready to go. There was suddenly silence. Bill introduced me to the audience, explaining what was going to occur during the evening. I then made my connections to Spirit and started the show.

The evening was going along brilliantly; there was lots of fun, laughter, and tears. I love tears, which are usually tears of joy.

Then, with one of the messages, I was connecting a lovely lady to her son who had passed. He had given me such clear information and she was convinced it was him, and this made her delighted.

"He is showing me a photograph being put into a frame," I told her. "He is telling me that he has seen you changing one of his pictures."

To which she replied, "Oh, yes, I did that only yesterday."

Then there was a sudden noise to the side of me and one of the large posters on the wall fell down to the floor. This made us all jump. I wanted to see what the poster was.

I ran over to the poster and picked it up, stunned by the picture on it, which I turned around to show the audience.

It was a picture of a photo frame that had a photo half in/half out, as though someone was putting a new photo into the frame.

The audience was shocked and there was lots of excited chattering.

But things were to get better!

We settled back into the evening and messages.

I had brought a family member through for a lady sitting halfway back in the hall. "They are telling me that they were an artist when they were here."

She was validating all this information as I was going along.

Then Spirit asked her, "Why are you not using your own creative abilities?"

She was just about to answer when again there was another sudden noise, this time on the other side of the room. Another large poster fell off the wall. This was too coincidental and spooky. Everyone was laughing at this point.

I ran over to pick up the second poster.

Once again, I turned the poster around to show the audience, and would you believe, it was a picture of an artist's pallet with brushes. There were screeches from the audience of disbelief. None of us could believe what had happened. Twice!

I certainly had not paid attention to any of the posters on the walls of this magnificent hall. I was too caught up in my nerves and what I was going to be doing. But how spooky that both posters that fell from the walls were remarkably closely linked to the messages and fell at exactly those times. Coincidence? I would like to think it was Spirit being very clever!

Again, such simple incidents, but very powerful with their meaning and validity of the messages that were being brought forward from Spirit. This surely would have touched and meant something to all the audience that night, whether they got a message or not. I am sure many would have gone away scratching their heads, wondering, "How on earth did that happen?"

The magic of that connection from Spirit is unfathomable. They try really hard to let us know they are around us. Why do we find it so hard to see these simplest of signs?

My grandmother, as I have said, was a tea leaf reader / psychic. People came from miles around to see her; therefore, she must have had a very good reputation.

My dad used to regale us with stories from his childhood, and this one really captured my imagination, especially since I have been working with Spirit myself and my wonderful Nana works alongside me.

It was the early 1940s and the Second World War raging. One of my uncles, Douglas, was the eldest of six children and had just returned to his depot from home leave. He was in the merchant navy, proudly serving his country. The family always found it hard when he returned for duty, as these were such uncertain times. Always hoping he would return, but never really knowing.

On this return journey, he had not been gone that long when, in the dead of night, while the family were lost in slumber, there was an almighty clatter. The whole household was startled from their sleep by this noise, and they all came running down the stairs, in the direction of the noise. My Nana was the first to descend the stairs, but there was no obvious disturbance or anything out of place.

Then, suddenly, she was the first to notice the seven white spots on the floor in the hallway. She stopped in her tracks, bent down slowly, and touched the seventh spot, which was apparently like a chalky substance. As she stood up, she muttered, almost to herself, "Douglas is dead!"

Everyone was stunned by this, as they knew from previous experiences that her predictions were usually right.

After a while they all went back to bed, as apart from these seven white spots, nothing else seemed unusual or out of place.

In the morning, everyone arose in their normal manner, getting ready for work or school, when suddenly there was a knock at the door.

"Who would be at the door at this hour?" Nana said. They were all a little surprised.

Nana opened the front door and there stood a very sullen-faced postman carrying a telegram. This would have been an ominous scenario for any family to be confronted with, considering they were right in the middle of a war.

Hesitantly, Nana opened the telegram, which, as she had rightly predicted the night before, read that Douglas, her eldest son, had been killed.

He was in a convoy of seven submarines and his, the seventh ship, was torpedoed by a German warship during the night. There were no survivors.

Nana and the rest of the family were all rocked by this information, although she had known the previous night, as Spirit had correctly warned her.

I was amazed by how Spirit was able to help me this day.

I had been home to the UK in the October as my dad was very ill. He was in hospital and had not been well looked after. He was unshaven, in clothes that did not belong to him, and when I walked in to see him, I did not recognise him. I was shocked to see him. He also had dementia, which made it hard for him to recognise me.

I returned home to Australia. Dad survived through the next month, and I rang him most days to speak to him. We had strange conversations, considering his illness but conversations nonetheless. He was able at least to recognise my voice and we laughed and joked about memories as best we could.

During November I was booked to work on the Gold Coast. The day before I was to start my work, I was just about to go to bed and decided to call Dad.

The nurse who answered the phone said, "You can't speak to your dad as he is not responsive enough."

I was fairly angry with her and told her, "Put the phone to his ear please."

I heard her muttering under her breath, but she reluctantly did as I asked. She put the phone to his ear. I could hear his laboured breathing and I said, "It's Val, Dad, just ringing to see how you are and to tell you I love you."

The sounds coming from him suddenly changed, and I just knew that he recognised my voice. I was saying my final goodbyes.

The following morning, as I had work booked for the whole day, I was up early. When my alarm went off, I checked my phone. It was 6.30 am and there was a message from my brother at 9.30 pm UK time, the same time saying, "Dad has just died". I could not believe that it was simultaneous.

When I got over the initial shock, I started shouting at Dad. Poor man.

"I know you have only just passed, and you want to have a rest, but I NEED your help, please! I have five readings today and I need your help to get me through them."

Little did I know how that would happen.

When working with Spirit, you really do need to have all your wits about you and a clear connection to the Spirit world.

But today I had just lost my dad. I was devastated, but there was no way that I could cancel my work at this late stage. I did not want to let Spirit down or my clients.

The day could not have gone better, and my dad certainly did not let me down.

The people came in one by one, and the similarities to my dad were uncanny. The same surname, the same Christian name, the way after only a few sips of whiskey they would get the punch line wrong on their favourite joke, came from Wales, loved Frank Sinatra music.

All these things were my dad. How clever are the Spirit world?

He had worked with me the whole day. When I got to the end of the day, I told him, "You can go and rest now dad and THANK

YOU." I felt truly blessed that he had helped me, and I had not let anyone down.

After each reading, I told my clients the story of my dad's passing and the connection that their personal reading had had with him. They were all stunned and very emotional.

Even though Dad was newly arrived in the Spirit world, he was able to help me immediately, working closely with me, bringing these magical connections and similarities. I will never forget this.

Whatever you do with Spirit readings, you constantly have to work things out. These next few were very interesting indeed and not what I had expected.

CHAPTER 17

Readings and How to Interpret Them

As I described previously, readings are such an important part of this work, on many levels. I love how this connection can rebuild someone's life after it has been destroyed by the loss of a loved one. Most people are devastated by the death of someone close to them.

A good medium can bring that relevant information through, to prove that their loved one is still with them, albeit in Spirit. Bringing through quirky, simple evidence that would be known only to the recipient. To watch the recipient's face light up and the love that radiates during a reading like this is the most wonderful thing to witness.

Sadly, there are those mediums out there who just skirt over a reading, not digging for the full meaning of what Spirit have to say.

I believe that structure in delivering your message is important. This will help both you as a medium and your recipient to understand fully what is being conveyed by Spirit.

I love the responses this brings from the recipient: "How do you know that?" or "Only I knew that" or "Only my dad would know that information." It is a very humbling experience for me.

Some mediums do not tap into the personality of the Spirit communicator. I feel this is a very important part of that connection. Our loved ones have a personality – describe it, become them.

If they were grumpy, for instance, they don't suddenly change and lose that grumpiness when they get to the Spirit world. Therefore, if they were grumpy, we have to tell the recipient that they were grumpy and describe them in that way.

A very important part of this work for me is the fun and laughter. Our recipients still need to be able to share the love and laughter from their loved one. We need to describe them as they were when they were here, an honest reflection.

I have seen some mediums on stage or doing private readings and they are very sombre and straight-faced. This does not fit with me.

Even though this work is about death, it is not all doom and gloom. It's about knowing that your loved one is still around, sharing their love, those precious memories, and helping us as they did when they were physically here.

Working with a medium gives you that time to share an extra five minutes with your Spirit-loved one. This is an exciting time for both you and Spirit.

Sometimes I have had someone come through from Spirit who obviously had sworn like a trooper when they were alive. Be careful how you convey this information. I was taught in my early days that it is not the done thing to swear in public, and I have always remembered this. It is being respectful of Spirit, your recipient, and your audience.

One of my very first teachers told us, "You could be bringing someone through from Spirit who loves to swear, BUT there could be a little old lady in the audience who has never heard any swearing ever, and she may just keel over and have a heart attack." I know that sounds a bit exaggerated, but it could be true.

I have never forgotten this, and to this day, if I have someone who comes through that did like to swear, I will say something to the effect of "Oh, they have very colourful language", or "I can hear a few expletives".

Unfortunately, I see too many lazy mediums who don't work hard enough to translate what Spirit give them.

I hear a lot of phrases like "I have a lady here, I feel she is your grandmother, she has curly grey hair, she was a lovely lady, she loved to bake and wore an apron, she sends her love."

How many of us had a grandmother who fits that exact description. But, if you said, "I have your grandmother here she tells me she had a wooden leg and a glass eye", that is far more precise and can pinpoint your recipient quicker. It's the detail in the reading that is the important part.

I had been teaching a course entitled 'My wooden leg and glass eye mentoring' in Sydney. I had a great group of students and worked them hard. The hard work really paid off with the evidence they were giving.

One day, one of the students stood up at a church demonstration and said, "I have a grandmother here who had a glass eye and wooden leg."

None of us could believe it when a lady put up her hand and said, "Yep that was my grandmother!"

The student trusted what he was being given and was confident enough to put that out to the audience.

These are two very important things to remember: to have confidence in yourself and to TRUST Spirit.

Working with Spirit is like learning a different language, and sometimes, as with a foreign language, we get a word slightly wrong.

If our recipient says no to something we give, we must go back, re-examine our information, and then, after checking back in with Spirit, give the information correctly. *Is that what I heard or what I thought I heard?*

The right interpretation is needed – what Spirit say, not what we think they said. The translation of the message could be completely wrong, and it has to be right.

This is a three-way process:

From Spirit (the Spirit world) – through Spirit (the medium) – to Spirit (the recipient).

In a reading, we have the medium's interpretation of what Spirit have said and then the recipient's interpretation of what the medium has said. We must therefore transfer that information as carefully and precisely as we can.

Interpretation of a word or phrase from each one of us could be so different.

When a recipient says no to our information, we must go back to Spirit and ask them to clarify what has been said. "Did I misinterpret this? If so, give it to me in a way that my recipient will understand please".

It's quite simple, just like having a conversation with a living person. If we don't understand, we ask them to repeat what they have said.

We need to be constantly checking in with the Spirit world as to what information is being given, and whether we have given the full meaning.

For me personally, Spirit will almost 'flag' a word, and for me that means I have to go back to that word and get the full meaning.

"What did I miss?" "How else can I interpret that piece of evidence?"

These are some examples of my own experiences.

"The lady I am communicating with had a balance issue."

"Yes."

I carried on with other information, but Spirit showed me the word balance again; what else could it mean? I checked back in with Spirit and was told,

"You are looking at your bank balance/finances, as there is an issue here."

"Yes."

Again, balance was given to me, back to Spirit.

"There is no balance in your life at the moment; it is all out of sync."

"Yes," was the response.

The one word was given to me three times, and I had to go back and work out the full meaning of that word until Spirit were happy that I had given the full meaning.

Another reading I did, I gave information confirming the Spirit communicator. She was happy with the information I had given.

Then, all of a sudden, I saw a "V formation of ducks" in my mind's eye.

"Hmmmm, this is interesting," I said to her. "I have never seen this sign before."

I asked her, "Would you understand or have a connection to this sign?"

"No," she said.

I could have said I would leave it but that is not how I work. If Spirit have made the effort to show me this sign, I had to work it out. This would be a tricky one, but I was going to try.

When Spirit started working with me, I was surprised by the cleverness of Spirit.

When ducks fly in a group, it's always in a V formation. I have seen this formation in the sky many times when ducks are migrating.

I told her, "It's time for change. You're feeling overwhelmed with where you are, in that lead role."

"Yes," she said.

Then I saw the lead duck drop back in line, in need of rest; someone else takes over the lead position.

I told her, "I see you moving from the job you are in – too much responsibility and pressure being at the top."

"Yes," she said.

Then I saw the duck that dropped back, the lead duck, move up the line again, but not to the front.

I told her, "You have been offered a new position. It's not the top job, but you are going to be happier."

"Yes," she said.

Brilliant that I was shown all this, and Spirit made me work hard to get the full meaning. I was determined to work it out. The lady was surprised and happy with the confirmation of everything that was happening for her, and that Spirit had been watching that closely.

She was in fact in a lead role, but the pressure had become too much. She was offered another job, not the top job but the head of a department in a larger group.

She now had confirmation from Spirit that this was the right move for her. It validated everything she was going through at this time.

I started doing the reading for a lady and her dad came through. He was a great communicator, full of love, fun, and great evidence. She knew instantly who he was with the information he was giving me.

He showed me himself beautifully dressed, but in his garden.

"Yes, dressed in a suit in his garden. That was my dad; he always loved to be dressed smart no matter what he was doing."

"He is telling me to talk about five pretty maids in a row."

Hmm, what are you showing me?

Then I felt I had a reference to the nursery rhyme, Mary Mary quite contrary.

I went back to the first line of this nursery rhyme and worked my way through it.

Mary Mary quite contrary

"There are two Marys in Spirit."

"Yes," she replied.

"But one of them was quite awkward, contrary," I told her.

"Yes."

How does your garden grow

"Dad is showing himself standing in his garden with very neat rows of vegetables and flowers. They had to be perfect."

"Yes, he loved his garden."

With silver bells and cockle shells

"He is telling me there is a silver wedding anniversary coming up."

"Yes."

"And you are going on holiday, not to the beach, but on a river."

"Yes."

And pretty maids in a row

He is showing me again five pretty maids in a row.

"He is telling me he had five daughters."

"Yes."

Spirit can use all sorts of ways to help you with your mediumship readings. Many times, they will show you an experience that you have had personally or something as simple as a nursery rhyme. It works for me and is worth trying if you are a medium. Always stretch your mediumship; never become complacent.

Spirit are amazingly clever, and I love it. As one of my teachers once said, "Never underestimate the intelligence of Spirit."

~ ❖ ~

This was another reading that took a fair bit of working out.

A lady turned up for her reading. We started and all was going really well. I had brought through a female friend of hers who she had been very close friends with.

We were sitting in my lounge, which had two cream sofas with a cream stool. On the stool was a blanket with black and white circles on it.

As I was giving the reading, I kept being drawn to the blanket.

It was odd because as I was looking at the blanket, it appeared to be covered in black and white roses! But there were no roses it was black and white circles!

It got stranger when, as I continued to look, these black and white roses turned to red roses. It was very beautiful but baffling.

They kept blending from one to the other. I knew this was significant but had to work it out, and with the help of Spirit I was able to get the full meaning for my recipient.

The black and white roses reminded me of Halloween. The red roses reminded me of a birthday.

I said to my client:

"She is showing me the 31 October, which is Halloween, and I know this is important to her."

She replied, "Yes, it was her birthday and the date she died."

"Oh, wow, she is now showing herself falling over and blood everywhere," I told her.

She replied, "Oh my goodness, yes. We were celebrating her birthday at the time. My friend was moving seats, she tripped over her handbag and fell straight onto a glass, which was on the corner of the table. She died on the spot. And yes, there was blood everywhere."

How clever again that Spirit could show all that incredible detail from the black and white blanket covering my stool.

~❖~

Another clever interpretation by Spirit.

I was in Brisbane doing a public demonstration when I connected to a young lady in the audience. I brought a family member through who she identified.

I was suddenly standing there with my hands at the '10 to 2' position. I knew this was the position you must have your hands in when you first learn to drive.

Then Spirit made me switch my hands. I felt like a bit of a lemon standing in this position.

I kept moving my arms back to normal, but Spirit just moved them back! Very odd.

I told the audience, "Hold on while I work out what Spirit are trying to show me here."

I then went back to Spirit and asked, "What does this mean?"

Meanwhile my arms were still crossed over in front of me.

"Spirit is telling me you are learning to drive."

"Yes," she replied.

"They are telling me while you were driving on your L's, you made a mistake. You swapped places with the experienced driver in order that you wouldn't get into trouble."

"Yes," she said, very sheepishly.

The 10-to-2 position was her learning to drive, and the swapping of my arms was Spirit showing me her swapping places with the driver.

This caused huge amounts of laughter from the audience. Again, how clever are Spirit to be able to show this to me.

Mediumship is a process, and each of us has a different way of working. But we do have to raise our vibration to connect with Spirit. Some can do this instantly, but for others it takes more time. This is called 'opening up'.

An experienced medium will still their mind, open their awareness, and put out the intention to Spirit that they want to work with them. Only then are they ready to work.

After years of practice this becomes second nature, or it should do.

When someone comes for either a reading or as part of a group session, their loved ones will already be there in the same room. They came in together. They knew of their need before they came that day.

Spirit is aware when we need help and will be there, very willing to give that guidance, some love from Spirit, or just a spiritual hug.

A good medium can bring out that physical touch and those words of love from our loved ones.

As mediums, we hope that we are working with people who believe or at least want to believe. If a situation arises where a person is aggressive, I will stop immediately.

I will do this for a mediumship show as well as a private reading. In 30 years, I have only had to stop a reading on three occasions.

The issue was that the sitter was not wanting to let me connect to their loved ones. I stopped these readings immediately. Was this their fear?

If you have any doubts when you go for a reading, you should talk to your medium and explain your thoughts and fears.

I always start a reading or a show off by asking people to be open minded. You are not necessarily going to get your Uncle John coming through; it may be Cousin Mable who can give a better message or is more able to give that message.

When answering your medium, it should be, "Yes, no, or I don't know".

Never feed the medium, because you are then doing the job for them. That's not how it should be.

The medium must make that connection to Spirit, who then give the information to you to forward to the recipient. It's a simple process.

I find it frustrating when someone comes to you for a reading and their energies are blocked. You can see them sitting there with their arms and legs folded. That instantly shows me their *energies are blocked.*

Again, this could be fear or scepticism. "Yeh, prove it to me, show me what you are made of. I'm not going to give you anything".

Some kind person may have gifted you a reading, but you may not be ready for a reading at that time.

A question I get asked a lot is, "How long after someone has died can I come for a reading?"

The answer to this is it depends on you and the Spirit. You certainly have to be ready as it is a very emotional experience.

The same for the Spirit person; they may want to come immediately or may not want to come at all!

When I look over my career as a medium, I feel the negative situations have been heavily outweighed by the thousands of positive experiences had, by both myself and the sitter.

I understand that connecting to passed loved ones is not for everyone. But if you don't want a reading, simply don't come. If you do come, then do it with a positive attitude; this will help both you and the medium. You may also be surprised by who comes through and what they have to say.

Mediums are not there to prove anything to you. We are there to share our love, our abilities, and our connections to the Spirit world, as they are with you.

The following chapter describes some of the difficulties I have dealt with in my long career as a medium.

CHAPTER 18

Obstacles I Have Faced

There have been a few obstacles along the way. This could be non-understanding of how Spirit connections work, language barriers, religious differences or fear. Some of the issues have also been around respect for me as a medium, my time, and payment for my time.

I travel extensively with my work. This is organised by myself, and I have been hosted and plans are made for me.

I would hope that the hosts would:

- make confirmed bookings
- make bookings in suitable venues
- book suitable accommodation if I am to stay
- explain to potential clients what it is I do
- organise transport
- organise translators if needed
- explain how Spirit connection works
- understand that after a long journey I need some rest time
- understand I need time to build my energies

- understand I need time to get dressed

- understand I need to prepare myself make those connections to Spirit.

This makes the journey for the medium easier, safer, and much more pleasant.

I have worked in many countries, some of which are not English-speaking, and I have had to work through an interpreter. This has had its issues.

Emotions or sentiments do not always translate well.

If the translator does not have an understanding of my work, how are they supposed to translate this verbally?

In one of these non-English-speaking countries, I was working with a family group who had lost a close family member. I had been recommended to them by someone who was overwhelmed with their own reading.

I was therefore under the impression that they understood before I got there what was going to take place.

They all turned up, and there was an air of anticipation, as is usual at the start of a reading. I could tell by their reserve they were all a little on edge and nervous.

Understandable. I was sitting there thinking, *I really hope that this has all been explained to them all, the process and what is going to happen.*

I tried to make them feel comfortable with some fun and laughter, but it was difficult doing this through a translator.

I eventually got my connection and was flying with information from the Spirit loved one when I was stopped in my tracks. Suddenly one of the group stood up and shouted in her language, which I could not understand.

The bit I did understand very clearly, however, was "Bullshit!" She shouted this as she stormed out.

This threw everyone and they all looked uncomfortable. This was very unsettling for me also. Later, I found out she had not wanted to be there in the first place.

There was a big argument going on in right in front of me. It was in a foreign language, but I could tell by the raised voices and animation that they were unhappy.

I stood there for a few minutes, a little numb. This had never happened to me before. *What do I do here?*

I turned and walked out. I decided to leave the awkwardness of the room, went to sit on my own, while my host tried to settle the family.

I could hear so much shouting. It was very uncomfortable. It eventually went quiet, after which my host came into my room and said, "They are all ready to start again."

At that point I had already made a decision. I did not have or want to continue. The attitude and the aggression had affected my energies. I was not in a good place to work anymore. With my energies affected, my connection to Spirit was not there.

My beautiful host was mortified by what had happened and tried really hard to pacify me but totally understood my decision. She went back into the room and explained my decision to the family. A few others came out to try to coax me back in, but I just could not do it. I felt devastated by what had happened.

When something like this happens, it's like your spiritual body has been 'bashed' and is 'openly raw'. It would take an enormous amount of effort to get back to that calm energy flow; I would have just been waiting for the next onslaught.

For a medium to work, they have to initially build their energies to a level of connectedness or oneness with Spirit. Staying in that sacred space with Spirit is a process that can be easily damaged or disturbed, making thc medium very feel very fragile indeed. Once that vibration has been affected, it takes a while to rebuild it.

I don't have to work in a space where I am not respected.

As a medium I am a sensitive, but I am also sensitive to the energies around me and if they are disturbed it's difficult to get back there, especially when confronted by a situation like this one.

I was very excited to be approached by an agent in Ireland who asked if I wanted to do a tour in Northern Ireland. I had never been approached by an agent before, which made it even more exciting. I said yes and all the plans were made between his PA and myself.

Off I went to Ireland. I had never been there before and was very excited by the offer of work and the opportunity to be able to visit new cities that I had only heard about or seen on the TV.

The day came and I arrived at Belfast airport, where I was met by the driver and guide. He was a real chatterbox with a very strong Irish accent and didn't stop talking all the way to the hotel.

As we were driving, he asked, "Would you like me to drive you around Belfast City and show you the sites?" I was thrilled, as you can imagine.

There were the ornate gates of the city. The glorious colourful paintings and murals that had been painted, depicting the troubles in Northern Ireland over the years. Although they were wonderful to look at, the sentiment behind them was filled with strong, hard, political statements.

These were quite graphic, showing some of the Bloody Sunday Riots massacre of 1972, the shooting of protesters, pictures of the hunger strikers, and people running from guns and explosions.

I saw some of the bullet holes in the walls from the riots. This made me feel uncomfortable, even though these events were many years before.

Some of the houses and buildings had chicken wire on the windows, obviously to prevent people getting in. This I found quite shocking. It was like being in the middle of a war zone.

This history, which I had seen played out on the TV news bulletins often as a child, suddenly became a hard reality as I was walked through those streets in person. What must it have been like for these people who lived under these regimes day in and day out? I would never know.

With the spiritual work I do, I know we are supposed to put a bubble of protection around us, so we are not affected by the negative energies around us. This however was draining beyond belief, and as much as I tried, I could not help but feel all the residual pain and memories of this beautiful city.

I was working that evening, and when I was dropped off at the hotel, I was grateful for the peace and tranquility of my room and to shed those negative energies I had been immersed in. I managed to get some rest before my first event, which was to be held at the hotel I was staying at.

It was show time. The driver and the PA were waiting in the foyer. They made me feel at ease straight away.

I was disappointed to find out, after having been told I would have an audience of approximately 40 people this evening, there were only 12 tickets sold.

When I started the show I explained to the audience, "I may only go for about one hour due to the low numbers tonight."

But I got going and the energy could not have been better. I was so enjoying myself.

I had given nearly everyone in the audience a reading when I caught the attention of the PA. "What time is it?"

I thought she was going to say my hour was nearly up and was really shocked when she told me, "You have been working for 2.5 hours!"

They thought it hilarious. I had been so engrossed in what I was doing. "We've been waving frantically from the back for over an hour, trying to let you know it was time to stop."

The time had flown really quickly. The most important thing was that everyone was happy. The feedback at the end of the show was fantastic, extremely positive, with questions about when I was coming back, enquiries about private readings, and more. All signs of a positive evening for us all.

The agent turned up after the show and we had drinks in the foyer. He said, "I was pleased that, although we had disappointing numbers, the feedback from everyone has been wonderful. I know the other dates we have set up are going to be just as good."

Most organisers come to the show and then leave you to your own devices. This evening was no different; the show was finished, and they all said their goodbyes and left.

Now what am I going to do? I was on such a high after a demonstration of mediumship, and now I needed to wind down.

I don't like going into bars on my own; I never have. Even so, I headed into the bar for a drink. The bar was packed, which was scary in itself, but I was relieved to see a man who I had bumped into earlier. At least there was someone to talk to. I had my drink and not long after I headed to bed, happy exhausted and happy tired.

The next day I was picked up at 6pm for the show in Lifford (Southern Ireland), the venue being the local cinema. The ticket sales for this venue were much better, 83 in total.

What a great night with great energy. Such a lot of positive feedback. "When are you coming back here?" and "Wow fantastic messages, thank you", and "I loved the way you worked".

I returned to my hotel after the show and ventured into the bar to get a glass of wine. This time I decided to go and sit quietly in the foyer on my own. No such luck, as two very drunk ladies came over to me and insisted, "You look like Farah Fawcett Majors!" I had been told that one before; I just went along with them and could tell I was not going to get rid of them easily.

On the other side of the foyer was another group of four ladies who had been watching my situation. One of them came over and ask if I would like to join them; I was very relieved to get away from the drunks. I enjoyed the evening with these ladies, lots of dancing and singing.

I still find it hard when travelling, as a single female, going into restaurants, pubs, or bars on my own. I know this is my chosen pathway and know that there will be many future nights dining alone, which I will try to accept graciously and thankfully.

I thought it would get easier for me but unfortunately it didn't.

My next venue was to be in Dublin. This was going to be a long drive and I was hoping to get a rest before the show. No such luck, as due to a communication breakdown we didn't get to the venue until 6.45 pm, and the show was to start at 7 pm.

What do people expect?

I arrived very tired. I don't travel well with other people driving, especially in a foreign country with a driver I am unsure of. The long and winding roads made me feel quite sick. Not a recipe for a good show.

I always try my best for everyone concerned, and this situation made me nervous.

I had been told that the numbers for that night's show were very good, which I was happy about. I was calling on all my Spirit guides and helpers for extra energy to get me through the night.

On the drive that day, my driver was telling me about a heckler that created a problem with another medium he had worked with. It was not a good end apparently.

"Oh," I said, "I have not had to deal with a heckler."

I realised later that this was Spirit's way of working and preparing me for just that, a heckler.

And that night, in my tired state, was when it was going to happen... Of all nights.

The show started well; the audience had a wonderful energy and was great to work with, lots of fun and laughter.

Throughout the show, however, a man appeared to have his hand up continually. I stopped and asked him if I could help him.

Heckler, here we come. He started shouting, "This show is rubbish and none of this is the truth! How can anyone believe a word of it?"

The driver was nowhere to be seen; I could not believe he had left the theatre! None of the theatre staff came to my rescue, either. *How am I going to deal with this?*

I told him, "With respect, you are entitled to your opinion, and you have chosen to be here and have paid for your ticket along with the rest of the audience."

He replied, "I didn't pay for my ticket I was given a complimentary ticket!"

He just wouldn't shut up. He kept interrupting all the time. The other people in the audience were getting very agitated and made comments like:

"We have paid our money and we want to see the show, so please shut up."

"If you are not happy with being here, leave."

"Don't be so rude and disrespectful to the medium."

At this point I asked the entire audience, "Are you happy with what I am doing?"

I got a resounding "Yes," and a round of applause.

One lady who had already received a message stood up and said to the whole audience, "This lady is good. How could she have known such accurate detailed information about my dad?"

Again, a round of applause.

He still would not shut up. I therefore said, "Please, sir, I am going to very respectfully ask you to leave the theatre." Very reluctantly he did, but as he left, he continued to ramble on.

"I am a journalist and also work on a local radio station, I will be writing about this shambles of an evening as soon as I can."

And he left!

I was very proud of the way I handled my first heckler.

I then apologised to the audience and explained, "I have not had to deal with a heckler before; that was my first."

Again, another round of applause. I was feeling happier and luckily was able to carry on with the rest of the show, which went very well.

I thank Spirit for showing me that I WAS able to deal with anything that was thrown in my path.

What an exciting pathway this is, eh? Full of drama, excitement, fun, tears, and laughter.

I was not bothered by the journalist's threats however, a few days later I had a message on my answer phone from this man.

He said, "I apologise for my outburst the other night. It was most uncalled for, especially when you were NOT the medium I thought you were."

This other medium he mentioned HAD recently been found out to be fraudulent, which had been blazoned across all the daily newspapers.

Most mediums or people working for Spirit do this work because they are passionate about working with Spirit and helping people. This is our life, our vocation.

I personally hate lies and deceit.

One of the obstacles I come up against often is about charging people. "It's a gift, you should be doing this for the love of it, for free."

In my early days, I too felt like this however, I remember having a conversation with one of my teachers about payment, when I was still developing my skills.

She told me, "If you call out a plumber, you pay him, and if you get an electrician out you pay him. You, as a medium, are being paid for your services. You have to pay your way in life. Spirit know that. But always have respect and do not take advantage of people's vulnerability."

She also said: "There is no value to your service if there is no value to your service!"

After all the years I have been doing this work, I still get people saying the same to me. Even when you explain to people how much training, hours, and money spent, they still do not get it.

Every other profession is respected for their time and effort – why not mediums?

Many years ago, I was invited by my London manager to enter a competition. It was called London's Best Medium. I did not want to go in for this as I felt very uncomfortable about the whole idea of competition.

Against my better judgement and with persuasion from my manager, I entered. It was a very scary process. I pitched up in London at this venue and realised that things were not as I had been told they would be.

I had been told that there would be representation from all the major newspapers, magazines, and TV stations. Not the case – there were a few guys with notebooks and that was it.

The competition began and it was a situation very much like X-factor, with a panel of judges and an audience. One at a time, we got up and did what we do best.

There were two groups. Each person was to be judged in their group, and the winner of each group went through to the final later that night.

Names were drawn out of a hat for placing and I was to be first up, which was very nerve-wracking.

We were all very different in our mediumship practice. What I didn't know was that there would be two fraudulent mediums in the line-up that night.

When this did come to light, it very much angered the audience and me.

The first guy stood up and did a fairly plausible psychic demonstration. He was last in the first group of participants. Before he stepped down, he announced that he had "duped" us all. He was in fact a magician and a mind reader.

I had a few of my own supporters there that night who had travelled up to London to see me. When fraudulent medium #1 was outed, one lady who was a client of mine was in floods of tears, very angry that this had been allowed to happen. This was all embarrassing and extremely uncomfortable.

Intermission.

In this intermission, she sought me out. She came up to me and, surrounded by lots of other people and still crying uncontrollably, started shouting at me.

"I came to you for a reading a few months ago. You gave me a recording of our session and I go to bed every night listening to that tape."

She continued, "I have been comforted that my dad was still with me and that I know he is at peace. Now what do I believe?"

Then she shouted even louder and with more emotion, "Who is the fraud? Is it you? Is it him? Who do I believe?"

I was terribly upset by this whole experience and devastated for this lady. I tried to console her, but nothing was working. This was terrible.

I have always carried out my work with dignity, honesty, and truth. I will never change that for anyone. I would rather walk away from my work than do that.

There was such a different feel in the hall as the second half of the competition started. The air in the room was subdued because of what had happened previously.

I was first up and before I started my mediumship I publicly stated, "I would like you all to know that I am very unhappy with what has happened here this evening. As a genuine, honest medium, having done a lot of hard work and training to get to this level, I am disgusted to have had to be subjected to this behaviour. I am also saddened and embarrassed for the audience."

The evening continued. The messages were flowing and some of these mediums were incredible. Mediums waiting to go on were stood at the back of the room, almost having our jaws on the floor by some of the evidence that was coming forward.

But something was niggling at me. Something was not right. I was not sure if this was what had already happened or something new.

The competition concluded, and the winner was chosen. I came second.

Spirit were screaming at me that something was not right. I was very careful not to make too much of a fuss at the time because I didn't want people to think it was sour grapes or that I was a poor loser. That certainly was not the case. I did approach my manager, but I was almost brushed off.

Spirit was shouting at me, "There is something very wrong here!"

What can I do?

How can I find that out?

I had driven up with others, and at the end of the night they decided to go for a meal. I had no choice but to go for a meal, too, then we drove home, thoughts of the night swilling around in my head. Why did I still have that feeling?

When I eventually got home, it was about 2.30 am. I sat down at my computer and started searching the internet.

I was not surprised to find out that the man who had won the competition had various plants in the audience. The three people who got readings from him in the second half were very good friends of his on Facebook. Their readings had been incredibly accurate.

This made me even more angry.

I shot off an email immediately to my manager and some of the others in charge at the event, but they would not listen to me.

As mediums, we are always dealing with people's emotions. We have no right to lie or make things up or take advantage of vulnerable, needy people. This is totally wrong.

I will always stand up for this, no matter what.

I cannot lie or cover up something, no matter what; I know that Spirit will work with me and trust that integrity.

A few months later this medium's title was stripped from him. I am not sure how or why, but he had indeed been found out to be a fraud. Spirit were right! My instincts were right!

These are just a few of the instances over the years that have taught me to be strong and to TRUST Spirit. These things have allowed me to grow in strength and belief in my work and working with Spirit.

I feel an obligation to recipients and other mediums, especially new trainee mediums, to let them know that this work comes with its obstacles, and you really do have to have a thick skin sometimes.

Some of the obstacles come from jealousies within our own industry, which I find really hard to comprehend. There is enough work out there for all of us, and we should remember that we are all different. Each one of us will offer something different to the many types of people who come to us for a reading.

I have had ample opportunity to travel with my work, some of which have been exciting, hard, or just pure scary. This experience was a whole mixture.

Up to this point, I had been invited to other spiritualist churches in the UK only. However, my first overseas tour brought such anticipated excitement and expectation.

I got a call from the tour organiser, who said I had been recommended to her and she wanted to invite me to do a tour of Turkey. I felt very proud of myself and thought this might lead to other bigger events.

I was given the rundown of dates, times, places, some of which I had never heard of before.

This was all new to me at the time. Not knowing how these trips worked out, I was pretty naive when I look back.

Excitedly she told me, "There will be so much work and it will be shows and lots and lots of readings. I will take care of everything as well as advertising." She continued, "Money earned will be transferred into your UK bank account," adding, "You will be looked after really well by the teams and your accommodation will be wonderful."

The last thing she said: "You will have a contract, which I will send out to you as soon as we finalise things. All you have to do is book a flight to get here."

There was also talk about work in other countries – it kept going and going. I really got hooked in with her sales talk and enthusiasm, at which she was brilliant.

I would also be working with a translator as in the main Turkish is the language spoken. I had worked with translators before and was not expecting any issues here.

Turkey is an enormous country. I had never been before and was not aware of its vastness. I would be working in many of the main cities, which covered a vast area of the country and travel between venues would be by car on mountainous narrow roads. I hadn't known this and didn't think to check!

After the conversation with the tour organiser, I looked on the internet at the beautiful places she mentioned in anticipation of this great trip.

I was in for a shock, that's for sure – in more ways than one.

It turned out that in each of the centres, I was to give the centre managers a free reading. There was usually more than one centre manager!

I was expected to do a talk explaining what I did and how it worked. I was told this was expected of me. All for free.

So far, two things that had not been mentioned to me. It turned out that each centre I went to would have their own agenda and sets of rules.

The organiser had told me, "All your needs will be met, don't you worry."

Some of these needs were medical as I am an asthmatic and I knew it to be a smoking country. I requested non-smoking work rooms and sleeping accommodation. This did not happen.

When I started working at the first centre there were only two readings, despite being told there would be *vast amounts of work*.

I know when I have hosted people myself, I take care of all their needs, making sure they have comfortable accommodation, a good bed, good food, and I show them the sites. None of this happened for me in Turkey.

The professional translators I had were lovely and they did a great job conveying my information as accurately as they could.

Turkey is quite a religious country, and most don't understand spiritualism. People were expecting psychic readings as opposed to mediumship connections. Therefore, there were a few issues with translating some of the terms or phrases, which we sorted out as we went along.

In each of the destinations I had much time on my own, especially in the evenings, and in the main, I was left to my own devices. I would have thought that a guest who was a stranger in their country would have been looked after better. But not so.

Most of my accommodation was very questionable. Mattresses on floors in yoga centres that were uncomfortable, in rooms that were being used daily for yoga. Therefore, I had to pack up all my things each morning. My shower was shared with other staff and clients at the centre. I had no space to relax or unwind and certainly no privacy, AND they smoked in those areas constantly.

I was surprised by no offer of showing me around or taking me out for meals, and I felt very alone and isolated. At the end of the day, I was shut up in the yoga centre!

I did have a key, but there were no cooking facilities available to me; I would have to venture out to local restaurants by myself.

Most of the centres were located in very rich money areas, and the restaurants were very expensive – and of course up to this point, I had earned no money.

Something I was not expecting was the attention of the Turkish men, especially being a blonde, single woman walking around Istanbul on my own, I was followed on more than one occasion. This I found to be very daunting. I did not speak the language and these men were following me. It was a vast city with lots of tiny back roads. My sense of direction is not the best. I had to learn quickly.

Istanbul had been the best place for doing readings, but it was still nowhere near what I had been promised.

Travelling between centres was by car and over great distances, as mentioned earlier. What I wasn't expecting was that on arrival, I was expected to just jump straight into work. No consideration for me at all.

"Are you okay?"

"Do you need a rest?"

"Do you need food?"

No one ever asked me any of these questions.

For me to be stuck in this very uncomfortable situation where the money didn't match up, nor the amount of work, the extraneous travel and no one who would talk to me about this...it was difficult. The organiser was just not contactable. The centre managers kept passing the buck: "We will try and get in contact with the organiser!" they said every time I asked.

Some of my audiences were a little hostile, comparing me to other psychics who had been there.

One reading was for a very sceptical man in Istanbul. He was a Turkish businessman living in Switzerland, home for a vacation.

The person who came through had been killed in a crane accident at the businessman's work site in Turkey. He was also a personal friend. He was interested to get this reading as there was an ongoing investigation and court case going on. Could he get any insights as to the outcome of the case?

What I saw was a crane, at the water's edge, lifting something up. Suddenly I saw the crane legs collapsing. The man's face was a picture; this sceptical man was suddenly interested in what I had to say, and he wanted more.

He was very shocked that I was able to give such detail regarding this accident, the man himself, and the fact that there was a court investigation going on.

There were some pluses to the trip, in that I got to see parts of this beautiful country. Istanbul, for me, was the highlight.

The streets were abuzz with people and traffic; it was much busier, faster, noisier, and bigger than London.

I visited the Grand Bazaar, which was the most inspirational place I had ever seen. The walls and ceilings were a mosaic of glorious colourful tiles, floor to ceiling of magic. I found it hard to take it all in. The smells of herbs and spices lavishly perfumed the stalls' fronts. The various traditional costumes the stallholders were wearing, no doubt from their own villages. It was an assault on all the senses; I was in love with this place.

Then I visited the Sultan Ahmed Mosque, also known as the Blue Mosque, which was exquisite. It was an incredibly serene place because even though there were throngs of people, a respectful silence and reverence could be felt. The walls were covered in hand-painted blue tiles that made me feel like I was cloaked in a healing shroud. The golden sunlight shimmering through from the domes high above me. I could feel the years of history, the passion of the people, and the layers of love.

Another exciting part of this trip was that I got to do a reading for the editor-in-chief of Harper's Bazaar, Turkey. She was so impressed with the reading that the next day she sent one of her journalists for a reading, who again was impressed, and they decided to do a story on my visit to Turkey. This was to go in the August edition.

A photographer came to take pictures of me walking through the streets of Istanbul. It was very exciting. The article was two pages with a beautiful photograph, the only downside being it was all in Turkish. But I was still grateful.

On returning to the UK, I eventually heard from the organiser. She called me and said, "This initial trip has been an experiment and we have learned a lot from it, but next time will be different and I have spoken to all the centre managers."

I sent her a very long email setting out my concerns regarding my work, accommodation, money, hospitality. She promised me that on my return I would get a better deal. I did not go back.

I told her this whole trip was one long succession of being taken advantage of. I felt like the hired hand, not an invited guest medium!

Chapter 19

Travel and People, Funny Experiences, and Apports

M any years ago, when my children were 13, 12, and 2, I had been given a message by Spirit. They told me, "Your children will be living in three different continents." I was really surprised by this message. I tried to work this out myself with my logical mind.

At the time, my eldest son had saved all his hard-earned pocket money to buy a guitar and was teaching himself to play and sing. Then progressing to writing songs and playing in bands. I naturally thought he would end up in America in the music scene.

My 12-year-old son had just won a book prize for helping an older person in the community and the book he chose was about sharks. His fascination for sharks was sparked from seeing the film *Jaws*; he was totally nuts about them. I therefore thought, naturally, he would be in Australia.

As for my 2-year-old daughter – she was too young to have any interests, but I did think we would end up in the UK together!

Well, I was very wrong, but Spirit were right! Again.

Yes, they did end up in three separate continents. My eldest son is in the UK, married to an English girl, and is still a singer–songwriter.

My second son ended up studying science, majoring in sharks and went on to do a post-doc in America, where he met and fell in love with another scientist and now lives there, continuing his shark research.

When I first made plans to come to Australia, it was not going to be a permanent thing, as I discussed earlier in this book. My daughter was around 18 at the time.

Little did I know that my daughter at 19, just a year later, would meet an Aussie travelling in Europe at the time. They also fell in love, and at 21 she followed him home to Sydney.

Spirit has a strange way of working. They obviously knew what was ahead for me and my family so many years ahead of time. I have said to countless people over the last 14 years, "I never planned to come to Australia permanently; it was only going to be a temporary back and forth situation."

But here I am and here I stay, and it's the best place I have ever lived in my entire life.

When Spirit tells me something is going to happen, I expect it to happen NOW!

But over the years I have had to learn a lot of patience as far as they are concerned. I find in Spirit there is no time, as such. Our time and Spirit time are totally different. I still have an issue realising this, but then I am extremely impatient!

Things will happen when they are meant to happen, and I have had to learn to sit tight and learn patience.

There are many examples of this happening in my life, but I think the most poignant one is being told I had to come to Australia. That took 12 years!

But now here I am, ensconced in a country that certainly feels like home. I've never felt like this about anywhere else I've lived.

My heart belongs here, and Australia makes my heart sing. I feel blessed that I was given this opportunity, that Spirit was right about this whole situation, and that I listened to their voices in my head. They knew – they saw it all.

What I have learned is to trust when Spirit says something will happen, it will. Then wait and let it happen in their time, the right time, when it is meant to happen.

Before we come into this lifetime, we are shown and told about our 'contract'. This is for the lessons we must learn to allow our Spirit to progress – progression of the soul. Each lifetime we move 'one step up that spiritual ladder' to get to the point of 'no return'.

I have read many books written by Native Americans; their philosophy on life and spirituality are very simple. That is what I like about it; it is understandable and makes sense. I have read that once we have achieved all the lessons, we are sent here, for our soul becomes pure and there is no need for us to return. We will have attained the highest level.

We are shown the parents we are going to and the reasons they have been chosen for us. I personally found this hard to grasp when I first heard this, but now I understand. Spirit could also choose for us what we need, not us choosing what we want. I think if we kept choosing what we wanted, we wouldn't get very far!

Some of these lessons we encounter are not necessarily for us, but for the people around us to learn from. For instance, when you have had a major event in your life, how many others around you have been affected by that same event? It makes people sit up and take notice. "How can we stop that happening again?" or "We need things to be done differently".

Other things I have seen include, for instance if there has been an accident, rules being changed in order that others don't have to suffer similarly. Laws are changed, monies raised, awareness has been brought about by an event. It's like a ripple on the surface of a pond, but in a very powerful and helpful way.

There are many more complex meanings to our lives than we realise. We only see a fraction of that. Spirit help us to improve our own world and the world at large as we go along. They can, as I have said, see the bigger picture, and they try to help guide us to do things better.

Sometimes it takes a reality check to make those changes. Being confronted with loss is a huge reality check. Why do we have to get to this stage before we take stock and look at what we have in our lives and how precious it is? We should really be doing this on a daily basis.

I, too, have had these wake-up calls, and also see it daily with my clients.

When things are shown to me constantly, it means to me I have missed something, or I have missed the meaning.

I had gone through several months of readings where a child had been lost. These readings can be very confronting and emotional for the recipient and myself, but they just kept on coming.

At the same time, each of my children had been going through various illnesses that could have been detrimental. I was extremely worried, and with this on top of the constant readings regarding the loss of a child, I began to wonder if I was missing something.

One day I questioned Spirit. "What are you showing me? Am I being prepared for something? Is there something I'm missing?"

The answer came from Spirit: "People, whether family or friends, come into your life for a short period of time, whether a day, a year, or a lifetime. But every minute of every day you have them, you should appreciate and enjoy them to the full. Cherish those you have around you."

That is what I did. I treasured every moment with my children, knowing that Spirit would take care of them no matter what.

We are not guaranteed tomorrow; that means today has to be special. Surround yourself with people who matter and who care. Love unconditionally. If it doesn't feel right, then it probably isn't right, so let it go.

We hold on to people and things that don't serve us anymore. If someone causes hurt and pain, let them go. Likewise, we don't need to hold on to material possessions.

There are times when you have no idea how you have accomplished something. I know that in this instance, if Spirit had not been right with me, the consequences could have been catastrophic. We see many such events in our world of superhuman strength. It had never happened to me before. But this day I was grateful for Spirit intervention. I believe Spirit stepped in and gave me the extra strength I needed.

My son Gareth had called me from America to tell me he had torn his ACL and needed an operation and three weeks of 24/7 care.

Without any hesitation, I said "Give me dates and I will be there."

I was running another business at the time. I made all the necessary arrangements for one of my team to take over while I was away and headed to the USA.

Gareth lived in the old Hoover factory in Atlanta, which had cleverly been converted into lovely apartments, but it was just like a concrete box. Everything – floors, walls, ceilings – all concrete. His apartment was very compact with one bedroom, lounge, kitchen, and bathroom.

His operation went well and he came home, albeit in a lot of pain and very drugged up. I was relieved that one of his friends had come home with us, as getting him out of the car and up to the apartment was really tricky. Gareth is not a small man!

We settled him into bed to rest, and eventually, his friend felt comfortable enough to leave.

I sat reading a book in the lounge, facing the bedroom. That way I could keep an eye on him if he needed me. I thought my son was asleep but was suddenly aware that he was out of bed.

I was on my feet in a flash. I was shocked as he was not supposed to be walking unaided. I don't know how he did it, but he got to the bathroom on his own. I was watching him like a hawk the whole time.

It was very strange, as the next few minutes played out almost in slow motion, but I know now that it all happened in an instant.

Gareth was coming out of the bathroom. I just knew something was wrong; my intuition was screaming at me.

I leapt up, suddenly aware that he was about to pass out. This was not good. My brain was working overtime.

I stood in front of him, using my whole body weight to keep him upright, pinned against the wall. Gareth was out of it in his post-op drugged-up state.

I don't know how and where I got the strength from to do the next bit. I was frantic and could not let him go; if he fell the outcome could be horrendous.

I was very aware that his bed was behind me, and I needed to get him on that bed. Gareth was barely conscious.

I asked Spirit to help me, and with a real concerted effort, as if I were possessed, I grabbed him, spun him around, and flipped him onto the bed, all in one move.

He was safe!

I know for a fact that Spirit was helping me; otherwise, how could I have got him on to that bed safely? If he had fallen, he would have fallen on the solid concrete and could have done untold damage to his leg and likely the rest of his body, too.

Thank you for that strength, wherever it may have come from.

The days went by, and he was getting better. He was still struggling with walking but could manage to do most things on his own by now.

After nearly three weeks of sitting in that room, we got fed up with staring at one another.

I had been scouring through the papers and happened upon an advert for a psychic fair. I said to him, "I think I should get out of your space for a while," which he agreed with. "I found this advertisement and think I'll give it a go."

There were many things I was not comfortable about with this idea – driving on the opposite side of the road, in a car I was not familiar with, in a foreign country however, I gave it a go.

I rang the number of the advertiser. "I'm a UK medium and happen to be here on the day of your fair. Do you think I could get a place?"

The man nearly jumped down the phone at me, incredibly excited. The day came and I set out with much trepidation. No navigation system, just a map. My worst nightmare. Me and directions do not go together, and I did get lost a few times.

I eventually found the hall, which was a quaint, whitewashed wooden hall, north of Atlanta. When I entered, there were rows of tables with excited readers waiting in anticipation for the arrival of the crowds.

I asked for the person in charge. "Can you help me please? I'm Val and I've booked a table here this weekend."

People seemed quite friendly, but it was obviously one of those events where the readers were all regulars, and I was the outsider. People were looking at me curiously. Who was this stranger?

I was taken to my table and waited for the crowds to arrive. Time was moving on and the crowds didn't come. The organiser was very disappointed and told me, "This doesn't normally happen."

What did happen next was quite interesting. People started chatting to me and asking who I was, where I was from, and what was I doing there. I told them of my mediumship background, UK training, and mentioned the Arthur Findlay College, which they knew of, and then, one by one, they all came to me for a reading.

In America, people who do readings, or at least at that time, were more psychic than mediums and they were fascinated with the way I worked. The readings for each of them were incredible. One of the guys, who is still in touch with me, was blown away; he had a special friend came through from Spirit.

"No one has brought him through before," he cried, tears flowing down his cheeks. "I am very happy, thank you."

I felt like a sideshow curiosity. I spent the whole day doing readings for the other psychics. I was exhausted at the end of the day, but I loved the exuberance and friendship from each of the people I had connected to. They were wonderful.

At the end of the day, I was just about to leave when the organiser came up to me and said, "We will see you tomorrow, won't we?" and "Thank you for today, it was incredible."

I got terribly lost on the way home, arriving at least an hour later than I should have.

Over dinner that night my son and I laughed when I told him, "I felt like the elephant woman in a circus sideshow."

It was a great memory and a fantastic experience for me, but I did not return the next day. One day felt like enough. Even though it had been a great day, the thought of the drive and the full-on energy work made me think better of it.

I was very fortunate to work in New Zealand and met an incredible amount of spiritual people, many of whom are still great friends.

Two of these were from the Auckland Spiritualist Church, David and Kathy. I was invited to stay with them for a time. They loaned me their car, as they had a spare, which allowed me to travel to various areas outside of Auckland for work. While I was with them, we wined and dined and did plenty of sightseeing. In a very short space of time, we became very close indeed.

One day, Kathy wanted to take me to Waitangi, where a Treaty was signed that is widely accepted to be the constitutional document that establishes and guides the relationship between the Crown in New Zealand and Māori. The Treaty promised to protect Māori culture and to enable Māori to continue to live in

New Zealand as Māori. I was intrigued by this, and as we prepared ourselves for the day, I could feel an excitement building.

It was a glorious day and we wandered through the beautiful grounds overlooking the Bay of Islands on the North Island of New Zealand, looking at all the historical sights and reading the history attached to it all. It truly is a beautiful place with a magical energy.

On the grounds is a building called the Te Whare Runanga (Māori Meeting House), where many performances and ceremonies are carried out with plenty of glorious food, 'Hangi', which is a celebration in itself.

The outside of the building was beautifully colourful. I wanted to go inside, and Kathy was keen to take me.

As we got closer, we could see a fair-sized crowd of people and a camera crew.

We tried to make our way into the hall however, we were turned away along with many others. It looked as if this special event was for select people only. How disappointed we both were.

Then suddenly, as if by magic, this very large Māori man came over to us and ushered us both in. Were the gods on our side that day? Was this meant to be? Did Spirit want us to be a part of this? What was going on, and why were we being let in when so many were being turned away?

We did not question his helping us, just thanked him and entered the hall. There were people sitting on benches; we followed suit.

There was quite a solemn air in the room; there were people crying, but it was all very reverent. We did not understand what was happening, as most of the people were not speaking English, so neither of us was able to understand. Kathy and I were looking at each other, wondering what on earth was happening.

Then the large Māori man stood in front of the crowd and started talking in Māori. He was extremely passionate in the way he spoke. We still had no idea what he was talking about or what this whole event was for. We found out later he was called Buzz Noble and was a famous Māori activist.

Thankfully, he then started to talk in English, and we understood that the people there were family and friends of two young men who had lost their lives. These two adventurers were part of an expedition of young Norwegian men trying to follow an ancient route from Norway to Antarctica however, their boat had encountered problems and these two were lost at sea.

Buzz was a very colourful character in many ways, not the least that his face was tattooed all over. The obvious passion he showed towards the young men he was there to honour was full of love and pride.

Another young man stood forward from the crowd to speak, again speaking in his native tongue, this time Norwegian. This whole event seemed to be very spiritual and solemn, and we were both very moved by the fact that we had been invited in. We were just soaking all of this up. We could feel the depth of emotion and love from these families in the hall.

The young man finished his talk, and then Buzz pointed to me and asked, "Would you like to say something?"

I was flabbergasted! What could I say? More importantly, why had he picked me out?

But he kept on beckoning me to the front.

I gathered my courage from somewhere. "Please, Spirit you know what is going on here, so can you help me?" I knew that Kathy was behind me, too, and we were both aware that something else was playing out here, and Spirit certainly had a hand in this. Kathy smiled her knowing smile, and I could feel her love, which helped me.

I stood in front of the crowd and started talking. "I'm not sure why I have been chosen to speak but am very honoured to be here today to be asked to address you at this very emotional, special ceremony."

I continued, "I am aware that sons have been lost and know this is a very spiritual, memorable occasion for you to honour these two young men. I am asking for healing prayers and healing for all here in this room today and for your lost sons."

"I know that your boys are still around you as they are in this hall today," I said, "watching and sharing this event with you all. They were brave, they did what they needed to do, and they are proud of their own achievements, as you are of them both."

I thanked them again for this opportunity and quietly sat down next to Kathy, who lovingly hugged me, knowing the gravity of this situation and the magnitude of the circumstances we had found ourselves to be part of. The energy in the hall was electric, emotional, and highly energised. We could both feel it, as I am sure everyone else could.

Then Buzz got up and said a few words in closing. The ceremony was over.

There were more tears among the crowds. For the families, this ceremony had been about closure. Their sons had been lost and were not coming back. They sat listening to the words spoken about their sons with pride. I could see the relief on the mother's face and the peace that engulfed her. We did not get a chance to speak to her due to the thronging crowds that surrounded her.

She did not speak English; therefore, the spoken word would have been difficult. But our eyes met briefly, and a smile swept over her face; her joyful smile and tears of love spoke volumes to us. She understood my message; she understood that her son was safe in the hands of God.

Kathy and I both had a chance to speak to Buzz, and again we thanked him.

Kathy and I walked away from the hall in total awe at what had just taken place. We talked about this in depth later that day, and we both knew that Spirit had meant for us to be there, to share with those families the love of Spirit.

I often question why certain things happen, and this day was certainly one of these days. Why were WE let in when others were turned away? Why did Spirit want us to be there? The words we shared were meant to be spoken.

Had we just happened to be there at the right time, in the right place? Our spiritual energy must have been shining very brightly that day, and that's perhaps what Buzz saw. He knew. Sharing our love and our light was enough. Buzz saw that opportunity to connect to Spirit, and that's why we were included. More magical connections to Spirit.

A group of us mediums who were all friends had decided to do some shows together. One of the shows we had organised in a local theatre. Ticket sales were going really well, and we were all excited.

What we didn't know was that one of the team had been working on a show with a TV presenter, Jane Goldman, who was investigating all things 'paranormal'. Steve had been asked to teach her mediumship as part of a ten-week series she was working on, and it had been hush-hush.

As part of her TV series, she wanted to show Steve not only teaching her but also demonstrating his mediumship skills in action. She was also filmed, showing her own mediumship skills at the end of the four weeks.

On the night of our show, for which we had a huge audience, she came along with her whole film crew. They were dotted throughout the theatre. This created such a buzz amongst the audience and us mediums.

The show started, and we each in turn linked to Spirit and passed those messages to people in the audience. Steve was filmed doing his bit, and when he had finished, they shut down the cameras. The crew had what they needed for the show.

Then it was my turn to connect to Spirit, and I was excited to be working for the first time with a psychic artist from Texas, named Elsa. We had met at the Arthur Findlay College.

We had a camera directed over her sketch pad, which was transferred to a large screen for the audience to see what she was drawing.

I made my initial connection and Elsa started to draw. No one was taking my information! It's always scary when this happens, but you have to have faith and trust that Spirit knows what they are doing. But this lady's description was pretty specific, her hair, the type of clasp she wore in her hair, the jewellery, and the way she spoke.

I kept going, telling the audience, "I know I am right; this lovely lady is adamant she is here for someone tonight."

It seemed like time had stopped; fear grips you when you think your message is not going to be taken and you will look an idiot. But I kept insisting.

Then suddenly, Jane Goldman herself put up her hand. The *only* hand to go up. She said, "She looks like my grandmother."

She then indicated to the camera crew to roll the cameras again as Elsa and I continued.

We didn't know it at the time, but this part of the demonstration was also going to be put into the TV programme.

Jane had been taught by Steve some mediumship skills, which she did well at. In the TV programme, she was shown performing publicly in the spiritualist church where Steve had been the resident teacher.

Jane was able to get up and give information she was receiving and had that information and message identified by an audience member.

Then in the programme she questioned what Elsa and I had done and said, including the drawing. Although after having been through this short period of training herself, she was more aware of how difficult it was to attune to the Spirit world and talk to the dead. It also showed her that many of us share so many similarities when it comes to describing our Spirit loved ones.

The conclusion at the end was that it WAS her grandmother, and she was very happy with the information that had come through. She also acknowledged how difficult it is to do mediumship and that a lot of training is required.

~❖~

I meet many people and have had strange connections with some of them. One year I was lucky to spend New Year at the Nariel Folk Festival in North East Victoria.

My early days had been as a folk singer, and I was excited to see all the musicians and singers and to listen to music that was warmly familiar to me. It was very hot.

When we arrived, I walked up to a lady near what I gathered to be a toilet and asked, "Where are the facilities?"

She replied, "This block of two toilets and the river."

I have never camped like this before; should be fun.

The atmosphere was incredible. A lot of these people had been coming to the festival for years and many friends were catching up with each other. One of the men had his birthday that week and brought all these inflatable rings; on the day of his birthday, people came, helped themselves, and walked to a designated spot on the river to float down the river to the end marker. I felt like a big kid, letting go of inhibitions and just enjoying the ride and the shared laughter.

I had been watching people around me and where they were staying. There were many mini concerts going on at this large campground. I was very familiar with a lot of the music. After one of these events, we all headed back to our tents, and I recognised one of the singers as a lady from a tent opposite mine.

"Oh, you're quite a dark horse," I said. "I loved your singing and that you sang many familiar songs to me."

She spun around in shock.

I thought I had offended her, but it was quite the opposite.

"I have been looking for a new stage name for ages," she said. "My surname is Horsely and that name, 'Dark Horse', is perfect!" she squealed with delight.

I was rather excited. I didn't tell her what I did with my Spirit work, just in case, as not everyone understands what this work is about. I didn't know her or her name or that she was looking for a new name, but I reckon Spirit did. Another right time, right place situation.

Later that day, this lovely lady was doing another concert and she regaled the audience with this story, and they clapped and cheered for her.

So many of us come to Spirit to ask for help, for many reasons. What a lot of you don't realise is that we have the answers to it all in our own hands. With the knowledge that Spirit is around us and working with us, to help us, we can access all that information ourselves. We just have to ask, listen, and accept. It truly is that simple.

There is nothing scary about any of this. If we are open and honest and always trust those beautiful energies around us, we will always get the help and guidance we need.

We must remember, though, that what we NEED and what we WANT are two completely different things. But the great thing is that Spirit knows the difference and will work to make sure our NEEDS are met.

I have many times done readings for people whose first language is not English, or their loved one from Spirit did not speak English at all. I love that Spirit translates what they are saying to me directly, in order that I can give the recipient the information their Spirit loved ones want to say to them.

It is incredible when I have been able to come up with words in their native tongue, when I have no knowledge of that language. It is not always easy, but I will say for instance, "They are giving me a word/phrase, which sounds like ..." To then see the reaction from the recipient who tells me, "Oh, that means [xyz] in our language."

I have been given names, places, and words that when translated are recognised, and that look of love and happiness on the recipient's face is magical.

Many times, I have been asked, "How do you do that?"

~❖~

Do you put things down to find them in a completely different place? Did you consider it could be your loved one trying to get your attention?

I have things like this happening all the time; these are just two examples.

I was busy getting myself ready for work, doing my hair in the bathroom. I had been using a big clip in my hair. When I had finished with it, I put it back in the drawer. Then, a few minutes later, I realised I needed the clip again. I went to the drawer, and it was not there! I muddled through and finished my hair.

I carried on with my day. A few hours later I went into my bedroom, and there in the middle of my bed was my clip!

How does that happen? Why does it happen? What was the message I was missing?

Spirit do work in mysterious ways, and I question them all the time.

Another evening I was just starting my live broadcast when something dropped on my desk in front of me. I didn't see what it was immediately but eventually found a button. It was a replica of the buttons on the blouse I had on that evening.

I checked all the buttons on my blouse, and they were all still in place. Now, again, how does that happen?

Is it Spirit having a bit of fun, telling you to pay attention to them?

Maybe watch your own circumstances. How do your loved ones let you know they are around you?

CHAPTER 20

Today for Me?

Today I am working in my business as a full-time medium and still get to travel extensively with my work with many overseas trips.

I am also fortunate that I live very close to three of my granddaughters and enjoy sharing time with my family more than ever.

The readings I do still give me that buzz – seeing the joy on faces after they have made that connection with their loved ones in Spirit. It turns people's lives around in the best possible way.

My public shows are wonderful, as I can make those connections in a public forum and love making people laugh, bringing through funny or silly things that Spirit share with me. Everyone in a show gets touched by the readings, even if they don't get a reading themselves. The information shared makes us all laugh and cry together. Tears of joy and happiness as the words allow us five minutes more to share with our loved ones from Spirit.

Teaching is still my passion, and just this last year I had two students who had never attempted mediumship in any way. They had read books about it, had an interest, and then found a workshop I was running.

Both ladies arrived separately. They came in as complete beginners and a little nervous, to say the least. I had 10 students that day, most of whom had been to some of my workshops.

All the students made themselves comfortable and I explained what we were going to be doing throughout the day.

I started them off gently to take account of the new ladies. In the first part of that day they both struggled to connect to Spirit. I think nerves had a lot to do with it, but experience has shown me that most new people, myself included, will be reluctant to put their hands up to anything in case they get it wrong. Both these new ladies are quite strong and, I have since found out, don't like to get it wrong.

I continually encouraged them to relax and enjoy what they were doing. The other students did the same. This support for me within a teaching group is vital as it helps us all. I also remind students that we were all beginners at one point, myself included, and that we should work with and help as best we can, the new students. I always share with students what I went through in my early days. How I got it wrong. How frustrated I would get. How my teachers had supported and encouraged me. It was important to remind them that I had been in their shoes once upon a time.

We stopped for lunch, and there was much chatter and sharing. The whole group seemed to be much more relaxed afterwards, and the atmosphere appeared changed. Then, along with all the other students, it appeared that the newbies had lost their inhibitions and the penny suddenly dropped.

They were both now bringing information that was acceptable to the recipient from Spirit. The evidence and sentiment being brought through and the level of accuracy were wonderful to hear. Both new ladies were both blown away by this. They kept saying, "I can't believe I just did that" and "are you sure you are not just saying yes to please us".

I love that more experienced students will encourage the new ones. I certainly encourage everyone.

These ladies applied to join my Intermediate Mentoring course, which ran earlier this year, and the exponential growth in their mediumship skills was beautiful to witness. They worked really hard within the classes and with the homework, which was mainly about the history of spiritualism, which they later told me has enhanced their mediumship.

In a year, these two have gone from strength the strength. As part of the intermediate course, all the students had to do at least eight readings for fellow students and submit evidence of it. This they did with flying colours.

I have been so impressed by them that I invited them both to serve a local spiritualist church.

This is always a bit nerve-wracking for me as there are so many things that can go wrong. But I should not have worried. Spirit made me sit in the audience, not next to the student as I would normally do, just in case they needed my help.

Instead, these two students stood, outwardly confident, albeit with knees shaking, in front of the audience. They both gave a prayer. They then gave a short talk, each choosing different subjects. One love of self and of others, the other compassion, forgiveness, and gratitude. They each only had five minutes to talk, and they covered their subjects with love and emotion. At the end, several of the audience members commented on how their talks had affected them, meant so much, and was just what they needed to hear.

They both did three messages each, all of which were happily accepted by the recipients. The description of the Spirit communicator and the evidence given when making those connections to Spirit was amazing. I was very proud to witness their level of confidence and the positive responses from the audience. There were many tears of joy and upliftment shared that afternoon.

After the service, there was an excitement in the room as the audience chatted with each of the students, asking questions about their training, which they happily shared.

I felt so proud of them both; after only having worked with me for a year, they proved that they had listened, learned, and were now able to put into practice what both Spirit and I had taught them.

I have many other students who are in the same situation, ready to step out and show Spirit they are worthy of being called a medium.

CHAPTER 21

Teaching and Where to Go From Here

I am grateful for all the experiences I have had, and I hope that by sharing some of these, you may resonate with or be inspired to consider working with Spirit also.

But now it's over to you.

Are you ready to learn how to connect?

Haven't found the right person to help and encourage you?

Sometimes that's all it takes is that right person. Could I be that person?

I was very lucky to have seen dead people from such an early age. Have you had something similar?

As a child I was brought up Church of England and made to go to church regularly. At age 13, I told my mum I was not going to church any more.

She was horrified and asked me why. I told her, "I do not understand the big words spoken by the vicar and I don't believe we are born, live the lives we live, learn all we learn, and in the end just die and get put in the ground. There has to be more to life than that."

I had never stood up to Mum in this way before. We did talk about it at length afterwards, but I stood my ground with my feelings, and she listened and understood.

This was the beginning of my spiritual quest.

Does this mean that maybe your own spiritual question is about to dawn?

Is your issue confidence, stepping out or being with the right teacher?

Do you have what it takes? Are you frightened of what people might think of you, like I was?

This is not a path to be taken lightly. It is a path of commitment, courage, dedication, and a desire to be of service.

My quest has become my life. I feel that is what a true dedicated medium is about. A life of service to Spirit.

Training

With my own training, I have had some truly inspiring teachers.

I am fortunate to have been teaching mediumship myself for many years and am proud that I can pass on some of my own skills and knowledge, hopefully enabling a new breed of mediums to work with Spirit and humanity.

I feel this is the ultimate aim – teaching as many people as possible to be spiritually aware. That does not mean they have to get up and work on platform as I do, but by growing their own personal awareness, they could help themselves and others on a daily basis.

I have been impressed to see many students who use their Spirit training in their everyday lives and jobs and how it has helped them to look at life in a different way. I have attempted to do the same in my own life.

Remember, you were born with a spiritual ability, and all of us with the proper training and encouragement can rekindle these skills. Also worth noting is that not every teacher is right for you. Or you may have outgrown a teacher; then it's time to move on and find another teacher who can encourage you to further develop your skills.

Personally, I may not know everything, but what knowledge I have I will gladly pass on, and if I see students getting up there and doing it bigger and better than me, I am always proud of them. I'm proud of them anyway, whatever they achieve.

I was taught a medium's role is to prove life is eternal, that there is no death, and the Spirit lives on. Lots of people go to a medium for a reading, but what makes someone want to do mediumship training?

This varies from plain old curiosity to "Can I talk to my loved ones, too?" or "I would like to be of service".

When you first start working with Spirit, it can sometimes feel like an upward struggle, that's for sure. At other times, it will feel as if you are leaping ahead. There will be plateaus also.

Don't ever be disheartened, and most importantly never give up; this is the most wonderful thing in the world to be able to do. Bringing light and joy into the lives of so many is an exceptional feeling.

You will be continually tested by Spirit to see if you are good enough. They will try new ways of working with you to find a more suitable way.

They will constantly be watching for your dedication and commitment. They need to see that you have the passion, as working with Spirit becomes a way of life, a lifetime commitment that isn't something you can ditch when you feel like it. They will also question your intention to do this work.

At workshops, I again ask each student what their intention is. If someone says, "I want a new career and earn more money," I don't invite them back. Clearly their intention is wrong. Why would I or Spirit waste our time and effort?

Your intention should be to be of service, to do the work of Spirit bringing peace, love, and harmony where you can. And more importantly to prove that the Spirit lives on; it is only the physical vehicle that has left us.

Spirit constantly changes the way they work with you. I feel this is a good thing and keeps you on your toes. They don't want you to become complacent, which, as I have seen so often, allows ego to take over. When working with Spirit, you need to be coming from the heart at all times.

I recently spoke to a lady whose husband was dying from cancer, and she wanted to learn how to link in order to stay in touch with him after his passing! I did not know if this lady had the ability, but I was willing to help her try.

Always be prepared for the fun side of Spirit.

I am constantly being challenged by Spirit in the way they change things up.

Today I will be working one way, but then the next day it's completely different.

I laugh at this now and just throw my hands in the air and say to them, "Okay, whatever way you are going to work with me, just bring it on."

Initially, both you and Spirit are learning to work together. Every time you connect to a different Spirit, the same thing happens. Like meeting a new person for the first time – are your energies going to blend well and are you going to understand each other?

Be patient, learn properly and do your best. Basic groundwork is vital and revisiting this from time to time is also important.

Mediumship is a similar process to playing the piano. You learn the notes, where your fingers must be placed, and then it's constant practice to be able to maintain the level of competence and improvement. All learning is the same.

Have patience and hone your skills – this will serve you well in the outcome of you serving Spirit.

Rome wasn't built in a day! Similarly, mediumship doesn't happen overnight. You need to go through the motions, and there will be many pitfalls along the way as well as many learning curves, some steep and some not so, but you just have to go with what they think is right for you, and not the other way around.

Over time, your confidence grows.

You learn to TRUST Spirit and work with them instead of being stuck in your head, in that place of fear.

Teachers

If you feel that mediumship may be for you, make sure you go to the right teachers.

Check out their credentials.

How long have they been teaching?

Where did they train and with whom?

Have you seen them work?

Do you feel comfortable with them?

Have they been recommended by others.

As with most things in life, there will be those teachers who you do not resonate with or have simply outgrown.

Is it time for you to move on?

Don't get stuck; you will do yourselves no favours by staying with someone out of loyalty.

You will need the guidance of an experienced teacher/medium to tell you when you are ready to move forward in that capacity.

One course does not make you a medium. What does make a good medium is years of dedication, training, and continual practice.

Spirit constantly changes the way they work with you. I feel this is a good thing and keeps you on your toes. They don't want you to become complacent, which, as I have seen so often, allows ego to take over. When working with Spirit, you need to be coming from the heart at all times.

When I first started development classes, it seemed like such a long, drawn-out process. I would get the sense of a person with me who was giving me their information, but then I had to make sense of what came next.

There are many things going on at the same time. It is not easy at the beginning. You have to learn to pull this all together and make sense of what you are seeing, hearing, feeling.

We cannot always get it right when we are starting out. It's like any new venture; mistakes will be made, but you learn from those and grow continually.

With perseverance and determination, they will become like second nature to you in time.

What were you like when you first learned to drive a car – the steering wheel, mirrors, gears, pedals! Yikes, remember how that felt?

This is just the same. Please have patience and know that you will get through this. Trust your teacher, trust Spirit, and most importantly, enjoy the journey.

When you eventually end up on platform, standing up in front of an audience, it will be scary. I have never forgotten that feeling.

A good teacher should be able to blend their energies with the working student and 'see' what you are getting and how you may have misinterpreted your information.

The more you do, the better you get. *Practice makes perfect.*

The Message

We must remember that connecting to Spirit helps people to come to terms with loss. To be able to say things that didn't get said when their loved ones were here on earth. To say, "I'm sorry" or "I love you." But also, "I am still here with you, guiding you as best I can. Trust that I am there with you."

People usually have a sense of humour when they are here. Just because they have passed to Spirit doesn't mean they have lost that sense of humour.

On the other hand, if a person did not have a sense of humour, then you have to describe that to your recipient accurately.

Delve into their personalities, even if they were a miserable/grouchy person when here, that information could be the defining factor as far as your recipient is concerned – just give it.

I believe that no matter what work you do in your life, it has to be done with fun and laughter, which of course raise the energies/vibrations and will help you to work better.

You are trying to build up a picture of the person from Spirit that is linking with you. This must be done in such a way that your recipient/sitter is absolutely 100% sure of that connection and who that person from Spirit is.

Most people come for a reading as they are wanting to know that their loved one in Spirit is still with them and that they are okay, out of pain, helping them, not alone, and still loving them. They need the validation, clarity, proof, which will help them with their grieving process and allow them to progress with their own lives.

There are those looking for confirmation that their loved one is now happily in the Spirit world, out of pain, still around, and they can still contact them if both parties want to.

We are not about 'doom and gloom', filling people's heads with negativity. That is NOT the job of a medium and again NOT what Spirit would want to do.

Sometimes the person who comes for a reading wants you to tell them what they WANT to hear, and Spirit will tell them what they NEED to hear. These are very different.

How Will You Work

Initially, Spirit will look at how best to work with you. You may not end up working as a platform medium, that is, standing up in front of an audience and performing mediumship. Some of you won't even want that anyway. However, there are many ways for Spirit to work with us and vice versa. So, give it a try and see where IT takes you, and not where YOU take it.

At the beginning of my development, Spirit worked with me on mediumship, psychometry, trance, automatic writing, and much more.

No matter what you want to end up doing, Spirit will have the last say. However, it is important to give every aspect of mediumship a try for you to find your perfect niche within this work. Whatever opportunity opens for you, try it.

Spirit want to connect with us and look for as many good channels to work through as possible. I believe this is to help the world that we live in, to help heal people, giving us all more hope, comfort, upliftment, and positivity.

If we work this way, we are working at a 'Spirit' level.

Psychic or Spirit

Just giving information and not identifying your communicator means you could be working on a 'psychic' level.

Take it from me, if you work WITH Spirit, it is much easier. They give you the information directly, you listen, you pass that information on. Whereas if you work at a psychic level you are trying to pull the information from the energies around your sitter. This is so much harder. Keep asking yourself, do you want to be a medium or a psychic?

Therefore, make sure that you are working at a 'Spirit' level, which is much easier.

You Have Been Chosen

There is always a reason that you have been drawn to Spirit. You may not know what that is, but Spirit certainly do. Spirit have found a common link and want to work with you as they can see your potential as a medium or healer.

We are all like beacons of light to the Spirit world, but some of us shine brighter than others. Spirit are able to see this; they know that the brighter, shinier ones are more inquisitive or have more abilities to learn about Spirit and communication. Therefore, they will most definitely want to work with you.

Also, once Spirit do have their hooks into you, they will not let you go. When Spirit finds one of the brighter beacons, one who can potentially work closely with them, they get just as excited as we do. It's like us finding a new, exciting best friend who has much in common with us, and we want to be with them all the time.

With the Spirit world, it's just the same. You are my new best buddy and I'm not letting you go.

This is an incredible skill and gift to be cherished. I still get very excited about the fact that I can do this work AND that it's such fun.

Always do this work with love in your heart and a smile on your face. It makes it much easier. Once you stop feeling this way, it's probably time to stop doing it!

Structure

The formula I was taught was CERT, which stands for communicator, evidence, reason for coming, and tying up the message. These 'rules' mean that you always know who you are communicating with from the Spirit world.

It is 'evidential' mediumship, which means you gain information from the Spirit world that is pertinent to the communicator, which leaves you in no doubt you have their mum, dad, etc. My recipients are left in no doubt who I am connecting to.

Every time we connect with Spirit, we MUST work out who is communicating with us.

Once you can give a description of what the Spirit communicator looks like, you then need to be even nosier, asking them questions about themselves. You have seen this in your mind's eye, or they have told you – how are you seeing/sensing your Spirit communicators?

Structured training makes your job easier. I was taught structure, and after all these years that structure still stands, as it works.

Responsibility

There is a massive responsibility that comes with this work. Something you say could affect someone adversely. You therefore need to make sure you are hearing and translating for Spirit, not making it up as you go along.

We are dealing with a person's emotions, and we should never forget this.

Why would Spirit tell you anything bad? They are there to build up their loved ones, NOT knock them down.

We don't know the mental state of someone who comes to us for a reading, and again, as I have seen personally, some of these people who go to a medium for direction will act on every word they are told.

Some psychics/mediums have given information that is totally wrong, and as a result, the recipient has taken their own life. We don't have the right to do this.

We, as mediums, are the channels for Spirit, and they certainly would not give bad information. I feel that this is something some psychics/mediums forget – it's not about us, it's about what Spirit has to say to the recipient, and they absolutely will want to uplift, help, and support those who come to us for a reading.

Do not go out without proper training. Untrained people can end up giving messages in an irresponsible way. This can also be very dangerous.

Natural-Born

Over the years, I have heard lots of people say, "I am a natural-born medium and I don't need to have training."

I, too, was a 'natural-born medium', BUT I KNOW that I NEEDED to hone my skills and to be kept up to date, kept on my toes with the latest ways of doing mediumship. This is not just for me, but my recipient AND the Spirit world. It is a respect thing for me, and I don't want to let anyone down. For me, being complacent is lazy and irresponsible. We owe it to who we are working with at the time.

No matter what profession you are in, you may start off with some usable abilities, but the only way you will get to the top of any profession is with ongoing training. Mediumship is exactly the same!

We are all born with mediumistic abilities, no matter who we are. Some of us will go on to use them and some not.

Therefore, whether you are a natural-born medium or not, the training is, from my perspective, very important for many reasons.

I get very frustrated when so-called natural-born mediums go out to do this work, with no basic training. They sometimes end up giving messages in an irresponsible way. This can also be very dangerous, and I have seen this myself over the years.

Protection

As a medium, you are a sensitive, and therefore you will be very sensitive to criticism. Don't leave yourself open to that criticism. Be true to yourself and to Spirit AND, most importantly, to your sitter.

CHAPTER 22

What Are You Waiting For?

Where Do You Go From Here?

If you have resonated with anything in these pages, then you may just need a gentle shove in the right direction. As I have said many times throughout this book, this work, working for and with Spirit, is incredibly rewarding and helps not only ourselves personally but so many others on a daily basis.

I would be happy to talk you through it, as I know many others would. I would repeat, please go to recommended people and centres if you have the urge to learn.

The only thing stopping you is yourself – so what are you waiting for? Get out there and learn. You won't ever regret it.

About the Author

Val Hood knew from an early age she had the ability to communicate with the dead. She will tell you that she never wanted to be a medium, but the Spirit world had other ideas.

Val has worked for over 30 years demonstrating her mediumship all over the world. She also teaches and is passionate about helping others to develop the best psychic mediumship skills they can.

At its core, being a medium is about helping people who have lost a loved one to deal with that loss and grief in a loving and compassionate way.

The healing that comes with this work is also a major part of Val's inspiration to continue sharing with others.

Knowing that our loved ones are still around us should be second nature – giving you that *Five Minutes More* to share their love.

Printed in Great Britain
by Amazon